SURPRISING SINGAPORE
● ● ● ● ● ● 101 THINGS TO DO

ORO *editions*

CONTENTS

INTRODUCTION	004
HOW TO USE THIS BOOK	006
MRT/LRT SYSTEM MAP	008
THE NEIGHBOURHOODS	011
APPENDIX	252
PUBLIC HOLIDAYS	254
GLOSSARY	258

INTRODUCTION

Visit the Lion City post-millennium and find a city in fast-forward. Singapore is on a roll, with a slew of new attractions and more to come after 2010. Shopping street Orchard Road has bumped up its mega-malls; nearby Sentosa Island now houses Southeast Asia's first Universal Studios theme park; and the Marina Bay area has catapulted Singapore onto the map with the Marina Bay Sands Resort and the Formula One Night Race.

In short, it's hard to keep pace with the Lion City. *Surprising Singapore: 101 Things To Do* brings you 101 ways to experience Singapore's many faces in its eclectic, evolving neighbourhoods. Here are activities to send you straight into Singapore's beating heart.

Locals call the Singaporean experience *rojak*, which means a mish-mash, unlikely ingredients tossed together to form a unique mix. We invite you to get lost in local neighbourhoods with a melting pot of races and cultures (Chinese, Malay, Indian, Eurasian); a mix of old heritage buildings revitalised amidst new boutiques, hotels, cafes and restaurants; a blend of a bold and more worldly Singapore, with its developing cityscape and first-world prowess; and slices of simple local life, like going round the block to a *kopi tiam** and having a *teh tarik**.

We also invite you to learn more about
Singapore's heritage, history, arts and culture
by getting to as many of the 50 museums as
possible. Collectively known as the Museum
Roundtable under the National Heritage Board,
Singapore's museums are packed with activities
and exhibitions which attract more than six million
visitors annually. To get you started, find discount
coupons at the back of *Surprising Singapore:
101 Things To Do* for entrance to some of
Singapore's most exciting museums (visit
www.museums.com.sg for more information.)

Flip the pages and get ready to go on
a 101 adventure!

HOW TO USE THIS BOOK

None of the extra stuff — this book is all about getting you up to speed on what makes Singapore tick. We've got 12 of Singapore's most interesting neighbourhoods and 101 things to do — just add in your own immeasurable sense of fun and adventure.

Just follow these three instructions to get you going:

__ 1 You love randomness. For an unstructured approach, just flip open the book, and try out whatever's on the page.

__ 2 Cover all bases by attempting the 101 activities in sequence. We salute you.

__ 3 Make a beeline for a precinct and get down to business. A perfect time-maximiser, or just a way to get the best out of a neighbourhood.

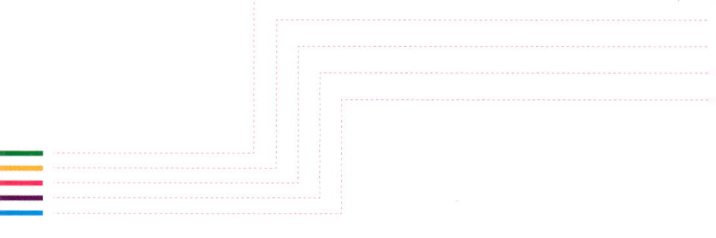

You'll find an introduction and a list of to-do activities in these Singaporean neighbourhoods:

- Orchard Road
- Chinatown
- Arab Street / Bugis
- Little India
- Katong / Geylang Serai
- Changi / Pulau Ubin
- Sentosa
- The Quays
- Colonial District
- Marina Bay / Fullerton Heritage
- Dempsey Hill / Holland Village
- Buona Vista / Alexandra

Look out for the codes indicated by the lines at the bottom left of the book. They'll tell you what type of activity each pursuit belongs to by the coloured bars.

- Wildlife and Nature
- Adventure and Sport
- Lifestyle and Well-being
- Culture, Arts and Heritage
- Entertainment

MRT/LRT SYSTEM MAP

The Singapore Mass Rapid Transit (SMRT) trains will take you to most places around Singapore, and you're likely to find it a godsend when it comes to getting around. On average, you won't have to wait for more than five minutes for a train. To travel, buy an EZ-link card from the station control; you can then top it up with cash value. Tourists can also consider purchasing the Singapore Tourist pass, which gives you unlimited rides for 1 day, 2 days and 3 days.

The SMRT currently operates main lines: the East-West line (green), the North-South line (red), the North-East line (purple) and the Circle line (orange). Take note of Dhoby Ghaut, City Hall and Raffles Place, three main interchange stations, in the central area, which will allow you to switch train lines.

We've highlighted the train stations that'll get you closest to *Surprising Singapore's* neighbourhoods:

- Orchard Road: NS22 Orchard, NS23 Somerset, NS24 NE6 CC1 Dhoby Ghaut
- Chinatown: NE4 Chinatown
- Arab Street / Bugis: EW12 Bugis
- Little India: NE7 Little India, NE8 Farrer Park
- Katong / Geylang Serai: EW8 CC9 Paya Lebar, EW7 Eunos
- Changi / Pulau Ubin: EW4 Tanah Merah
- Sentosa: NE1 Harbourfront
- The Quays: NE5 Clarke Quay, EW13 NS25 City Hall,
- Colonial District: EW13 NS25 City Hall, CC2 Bras Basah, CC3 Esplanade, CC4 Promenade, NS24 NE6 CC1 Dhoby Ghaut
- Marina Bay / Fullerton Heritage: NS27 Marina Bay, NS26 EW14 Raffles Place
- Dempsey Hill / Holland Village: NS22 Orchard, EW21 Buona Vista
- Buona Vista / Alexandra: EW21 Buona Vista, EW20 Commonwealth, NE1 Harbourfront

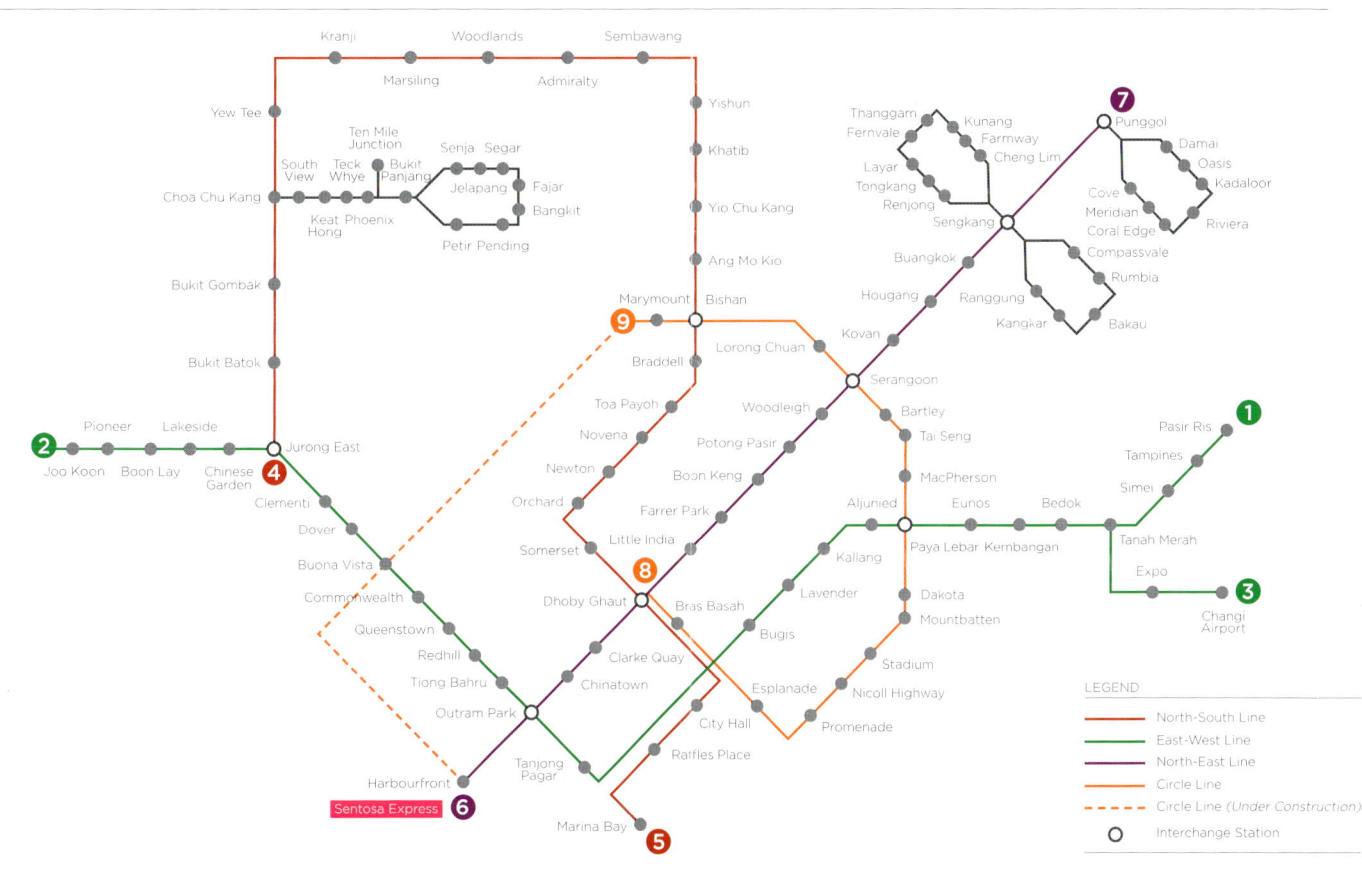

THE NEIGHBOURHOODS

ORCHARD ROAD

Catch Singaporean films at Sinema Old School	020
Steal a moment at Emerald Hill	022
Buy ice cream from a road-side stall	024
Experience Borsch, Alaskas, skewers and old-world class at Shashlik	025
Picnic at the Singapore Botanic Gardens	026
Get all spa-ed out in town	028

CHINATOWN

Enjoy traditional Chinese pastries at Tong Heng Confectionery	038
Discover Singapore's first street museum, Fuk Tak Chi Museum	040
Go hunting for collectibles	042
Wander Ann Siang Road and Club Street	044
Watch Chinese opera at the Chinese Opera Teahouse	046
Unravel Chinatown's history at the Chinatown Heritage Centre	048
Think design at the red dot design museum	050
Discover the Buddha Tooth Relic Temple and Museum	052
Visit the Sri Mariamman Temple	054
Discover Peranakan heritage at the Baba House	056
Catch wet market scenes on Smith Street	058
Feast on local favourite, satay, at Lau Pa Sat	060
Discover the Singapore General Hospital Museum	062
Have traditional dim sum at Red Star Restaurant	064

ARAB STREET/BUGIS

Pick up cool threads at Blackmarket	073
Look up independent boutiques at Haji Lane	074
Go street shopping at Bugis Village Street Bazaar	076
Relive childhood memories at the Mint Museum of Toys	078
Get your underground music fix at Straits Records	079
Bibliophiles, seek relief at the National Library Building	080
Puff the magic dragon: Shisha	081
Shopaholics, buy ethnic curios from Arab Street	082
Eat your way around the world... Around Arab Street	084
Visit a slice of history at the Malay Heritage Centre	086

LITTLE INDIA

Burn the midnight oil shopping at Mustafa Centre	094
Indulge in a roti prata and teh tarik	096
Go vegan (and do good) at Food #03	097
Dig for treasure at Sungei Road Thieves Market	098
Visit the Land Transport Gallery	100
To shelter! To shelter! In Sri Veeramakaliamman Temple	101
Mind your leafware manners! Or banana leaves as plates	102
Visit Little India Arcade: The place for all things Indian	104
Consult Mani the parakeet who sees all, picks all	106
Celebrate life with Henna tatoos	107

KATONG/GEYLANG SERAI

Gorge yourself on a Katong food trail	114
Admire the architecture of Joo Chiat's Peranakan houses	116
Go on a tour of Peranakan heritage at Katong Antique House	118
Visit the Sri Senpaga Vinayagar Temple	120
Celebrate a living artist at the Tan Swie Hian Museum	121
Soak in the atmosphere at Geylang Serai Market & Food Centre	122
Go ethnic shopping at Joo Chiat Complex	124
Try nasi padang	125

CHANGI/PULAU UBIN

Queue up for nasi lemak	132
Recount the war years at Changi Chapel and Museum	133
Nature walk at Chek Jawa	134
Cycle around Pulau Ubin	136
Get some lovin' on the Changi Point Coastal Walk	137
Gorge on fresh seafood on Pulau Ubin	138
Whip up a feast... in Pulau Ubin's jungle	139

SENTOSA

Catch a cable car ride	146
Get fish foot therapy at Underwater World	147
Go on a big day out at Resorts World Sentosa	148
Pump, jump, spike and surf at Sentosa's beaches	150
Release your inner kid on the Sentosa Luge	152
Visit Images of Singapore	153

THE QUAYS

Party at Zouk	160
Go bar-hopping at Clarke Quay	161
Hang out at board game cafes	162
Dine at Robertson Quay's restaurants	164
Marvel contemporary prints at the Singapore Tyler Print Institute	166
Bumboat down the Singapore River	167

COLONIAL DISTRICT

Take your kids to a fire station at the Civil Defence Heritage Gallery	175
Get a 101 on Singapore's history at the National Museum of Singapore	176
Take a trip in time at the Battle Box	178
Discover the Singapore Philatelic Museum	179
Catch the Asian art bug at Singapore Art Museum	180
Discover Asian history at the Asian Civilisations Museum	182
Discover ethnic flavours at the Peranakan Museum	184
Take a leisurely stroll at Fort Canning Park	186
Catch experimental art at the Substation	187
Grab a Singapore Sling at Raffles Hotel	188
Get on top of the city at rooftop bars	189
Have romance on the lawn at Chijmes	190
Take a ride in a trishaw	192
See a show at the Esplanade	193
Go for late night supper at Makansutra Gluttons Bay	194

MARINA BAY / FULLERTON HERITAGE

Enjoy the water views at Marina Barrage	202
Be awed by the Marina Bay Sands Integrated Resort	204
Party at the Butter Factory	206
Fly the Singapore Flyer	207
Catch the Singapore Formula One Night Race	208
Wine and dine at the Fullerton Heritage	210

DEMPSEY HILL / HOLLAND VILLAGE

Enjoy Sunday brunch at Dempsey Hill	220
Get a beauty fix at HOUSE's Beauty Emporium	222
Hit late-night bars at intimate Dempsey Hill	224
Wander around Holland Road Shopping Centre	226
Wine, dine and relax at Chip Bee Gardens	227
Live well at Phoenix Park	228

BUONA VISTA / ALEXANDRA

Go back in time at Colbar	236
Visit artist hideaways in the wild at Wessex Estate	238
Dine in a secret garden at Rochester Park and Portsdown Road	240
Spend afternoons at the gardens at HortPark	242
Hike on the Southern Ridges	244
Remember our wartime dead at Reflections at Bukit Chandu	246
Explore Singapore's 'Cu Chi tunnels' at Labrador Nature Reserve	248

ORCHARD ROAD

London has Oxford Street, New York has Fifth Avenue — when in Singapore, the street name that'll stick in your mind is Orchard Road. Beginning at Tanglin Road and ending at Dhoby Ghaut, locals might complain how it appears that the whole of Singapore seems to pack the Orchard area on the weekends (read: it's that crowded), but that's just part of the whole Orchard Road experience.

On street level, you'll find the flagship stores of the "who's who" of international brands rubbing shoulders in a no-holds-barred display of opulence. Orchard Road is unabashedly mall-dominated; its latest luminaries include ION Orchard, the street's most iconic shopping mall; 313@Somerset, home to popular brands Forever 21, Uniqlo and Zara; and Mandarin Gallery, with its list of carefully curated stores and offerings that'll make you feel like a VIP strolling its narrow halls.

Orchard Road may not be conquered in a day — and you may find yourself coming back to its many stores, restaurants, movie theatres and cafes just to feel the city's buzz. But even Orchard Road has its little niches in and around the main street; for a dose of alternative Orchard Road, read on.

THE SPOTS

__ 1 ALLEY BAR
180 Orchard Road
Peranakan Place
Singapore 238846
Tel: 6738 8818
www.peranakanplace.com/alleybar.html

__ 2 ESTHEVA SPA
2 Orchard Turn
#03-25, ION Orchard
Singapore 238801
Tel: 6509 3900
www.estheva.com

__ 3 ICE COLD BEER
9 Emerald Hill Road
Singapore 229293
Tel: 6735 9929
icb.emerald-hill.com

__ 4 NO. 5 EMERALD HILL COCKTAIL BAR
5 Emerald Hill Rd
Singapore 229289
Tel: 6732 0818

__ 5 REMÈDE SPA,
THE ST REGIS SINGAPORE
29 Tanglin Road
Singapore 247911
Tel: 6506 6896
www.stregissingapore.com/spa

__ 6 SHASHLIK RESTAURANT
545 Orchard Road
#06-19, Far East Shopping Centre
Singapore 238882
Tel: 6732 6401

__ 7 SINEMA OLD SCHOOL
11B Mount Sophia
#B1-12, Old School
Singapore 228466
Tel: 6336 9707
www.sinema.sg

__ 8 SINGAPORE BOTANIC GARDENS
1 Cluny Road
Singapore 259569
Tel: 6471 7138 / 6471 7361
www.sbg.org.sg

__ 9 SPA BOTANICA (TANGLIN CLUB)
The Tanglin Club
5 Stevens Road
Singapore 257814
Tel: 6371 1318
www.spabotanica.com

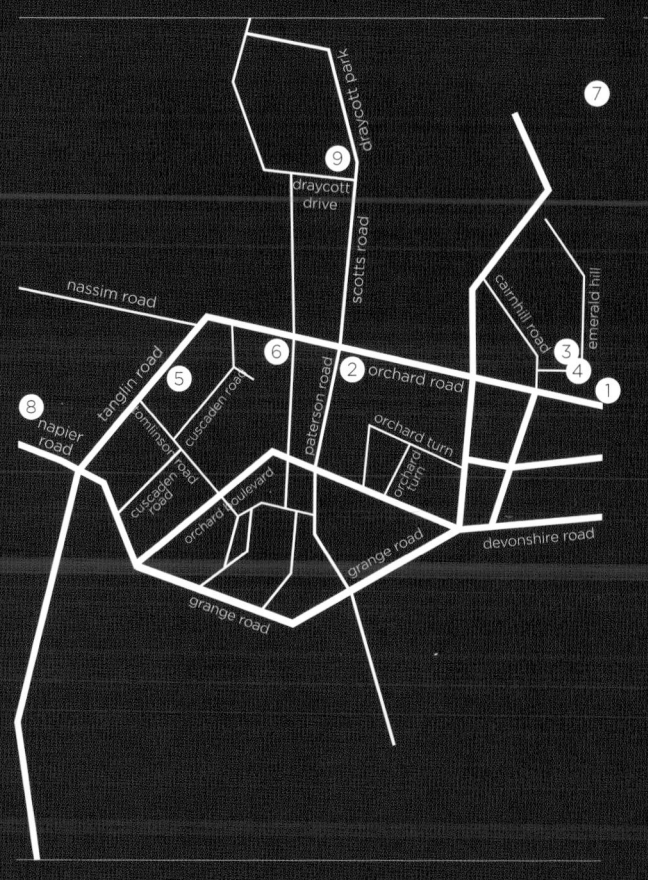

CHECK OUT

Sinema's website, www.sinema.sg, for the latest screenings across Asian, Asian-American, UK, Singapore and social films.

CATCH SINGAPOREAN FILMS AT SINEMA OLD SCHOOL

First, the bad news: to get to Sinema @ Old School on foot, be prepared for a mini-vertical marathon up 137 flights of stairs behind Dhoby Ghaut station. Trust us, the trek uphill is well worth the exercise. In the not-so-far horizon across Mount Sophia Road sits Old School — *literally*, as the building was once the Methodist Girls' School — a cooler-than-thou sanctuary for Singapore's creative community, or as a headline on the building façade declares, this place houses digs for new-school thinkers.

Enter Sinema at the basement of this white-washed building for one of *the* best places to catch Singaporean films from up-and-coming directors. Sinema's mission should be obvious by now (yes, it's a play between Singapore and cinema) — this is where the next big director may very well have his first modest screening. The cinema is unabashedly indie, with a modest wooden bench downstairs where late-night discussions on Singapore's film future are sparked, a small store selling film memorabilia and a cosy 136-seat theatre. For the latest screenings across Asian, Asian-American, UK, Singapore and social films, head to www.sinema.sg. While you're here, take a peek into the offices of a slew of hip advertising and design companies on the upper levels.

STEAL A MOMENT AT EMERALD HILL

Quiet spaces in busy Orchard Road are as incongruous as ice cream on bread. But they exist like said ice cream sandwiches. In fact, a popular quiet space is in a blink-and-you'd-miss-it cobblestoned alleyway that's directly opposite shopping mall 313@Somerset.

The alleyway opens up into a collection of Peranakan-styled shophouses and gardens with swings and seesaws from a bygone era. It's just perfect for architectural buffs who are into gems of history.

Come nightfall, Emerald Hill fills up with laughing people drinking at No. 5 Emerald Hill Cocktail Bar, which offers stylish cocktails and chilli vodka shots, or Alley Bar, with its narrow-as-a-model's-waist space, or Ice Cold Beer for beers from around the world.

LOOK FOR

A cobblestoned alleyway opposite 313@Somerset to admire quaint shophouses or get a beer at a bar.

BUY ICE CREAM FROM A ROAD-SIDE STALL

As locals might nostalgically tell you, there was a time in Singapore when snacks cost a mere 20 cents, enough to delight little children on a hot afternoon. With rising costs of living, what locals call "cheap and good" treats are no longer what they used to be in the 70's and 80's. Yet, on urbanised Orchard Road, you'll still be able to find a throwback to the simple life with roadside vendors selling ice cream.

You'll recognise these ice cream vendors by their mobile stalls, complete with a tin box attached to a motorbike. Buy a scoop of ice cream at a steal for only S$1 (or slightly more) — it's enough to perk you up when the afternoon heat gets to you. Try the wholesome ice cream flavours, from local favourites red-bean, durian and coconut, to chocolate and blueberry. To eat the ice cream the local way, ask for a scoop between a slice of rainbow-coloured bread.

DID YOU

Eat ice cream the local way — between a slice of rainbow-coloured bread?

EXPERIENCE BORSCH, ALASKAS, SKEWERS AND OLD-WORLD CLASS AT SHASHLIK

DID YOU

Marvel the survival of this old-school Russian-Hanainese restaurant on swanky Orchard Road?

This Russian restaurant (with a heavy dose of *Hainanese** flavour) has been around since 1986. It looks the part too, with dim interiors, cheap wooden tables and chairs, and matronly waitresses.

In fact, Shashlik has survived for this long at Far East Shopping Centre on the backs of their Borsch, Bomb Alaska, and Beef Shashlik dishes. All three dishes are shoo-ins according to their customers, who include nostalgic grandparents as well as the young 'uns.

You might especially like how they present their food. It comes on a trolley that is pushed up to your table by a dour-faced waitress who either slings meat off a skewer or sets a puffy meringue on fire. And while you're waiting for your meal to sizzle or light up, remember to drink up the old-school-almost-colonial atmosphere.

WE RECOMMEND

Taking your pick of picnic spots around three beautiful lakes.

Visiting the Jacob Ballas Children Garden with its interactive play spots.

PICNIC AT THE SINGAPORE BOTANIC GARDENS

A stone's throw away from Orchard Road, and open all year from 5am to 12 midnight, there's little reason not to enjoy the tranquil landscaped gardens of the Singapore Botanic Gardens. Whether you're going solo, as a couple or as a family, there are spots aplenty to enjoy a picnic, curl up over a good book, and admire the beauty of tropical plants.

Take your pick of picnic spots around three beautiful lakes: Swan Lake, known for mute swans from Amsterdam; the Symphony Lake, which occasionally holds open-air concerts at the Shaw Foundation Symphony Stage; and Eco-Lake, where you can admire black swans, migrant ducks, herons and water hens. The Jacob Ballas Children's Garden is a great location to teach kids about nature, with interactive play spots and shelters under which to unpack your sandwiches. Otherwise, there are various wide-open spaces around the grounds to lay a mat and relax.

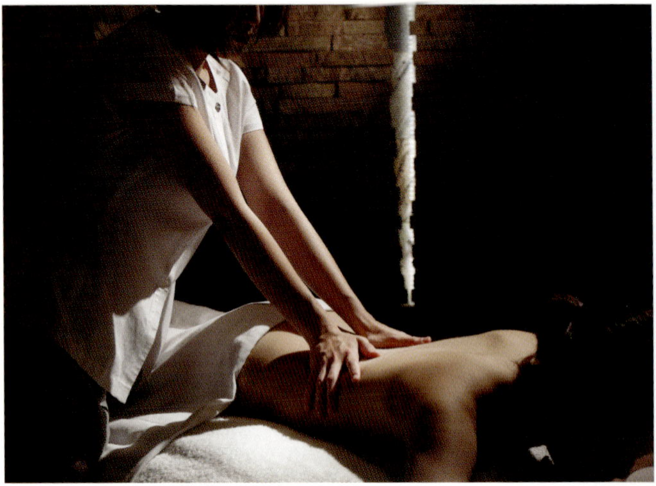

ORCHARD ROAD

YOU MUST TRY

A signature massage or beauty treatment from Orchard Road's best spas.

GET ALL SPA'ED OUT IN TOWN

1

A bout of spa pampering on Orchard Road is no ordinary affair. These urban oases have signature massages, beauty treatments and body wraps galore — along with the fine touches that will make your spa session exceptional.

Like the signature Warm Jade Stone Massage at Remède Spa on level two of six-star hotel, The St Regis Singapore; or a body wrap in scented Rassoul mud that moisturises your skin as you lie on a mildly heated marble slab. ESTHEVA Spa at ION Orchard has been making headlines as a top day spa. It's all about pure indulgence and results, be it getting your body drizzled with pure chocholate to fight aging, or exfoliating the skin with a seaweed scrub chockfull of minerals.

Over at the Tanglin Club, the award-winning Spa Botanica is all about natural therapies, be it cooling your skin with yoghurt with the Balinese Spice Retreat, or flushing out body toxins with healing clay fortified by lotus blossoms and ginseng in the Five Elements Cleansing and Purifying Ritual.

1.2.4. Remède Spa (Images courtesy of Remède Spa, The St Regis Singapore)
3.5. ESTHEVA Spa

CHINATOWN

Chinatown could well be one of your first stops in Singapore — and rightly so. The buzzword of the area is history, from the *five-foot ways** where Chinese coolies and hawkers populate, to the 20th century architectural landmarks and the ubiquitous street fare.

But Singapore has an appetite for reinvention, and Chinatown is one of its golden boys. The old bullock carts that gave the area its old moniker, *Niu Che Shui** (roughly translated as Bullock Cart Water), no longer parade the streets. This is Chinatown's 21st century face: a place where progressive retail stores, chic boutique hotels, modern offices, museums and restaurants have struck a happy alliance with the area's heritage to bring you culture *du jour*.

Along Eu Tong Sen Street, you'll find most of the bigger complexes including People's Park Complex, a former opera house turned shopping mall, Majestic Theatre and Pearl's Centre. The trail-worthy areas are opposite around Chinatown MRT, all the way from Upper Cross Street to Bukit Pasoh Road. Pagoda Street and Temple Street form the usual tourist stretch, with their souvenir stores and jazzed-up food joints. But Chinatown is compact enough for you to wander off the usual spots and still get back on track for lunch-time. For the one-offs exclusive to the un-missable Chinatown, read on.

THE SPOTS

__ 1 BABA HOUSE
157 Neil Road
Singapore 088883
Tel: 6227 5731
www.nus.edu.sg/museum/baba

__ 2 BEAUJOLAIS WINE BAR
1 Ann Siang Hill
Singapore 069784
Tel: 6224 2227

__ 3 BOOKS ACTUALLY /
POLYMATH & CRUST
86 Club Street
Singapore 069454
Tel: 6222 9195
www.booksactually.com

__ 4 BUDDHA TOOTH RELIC
TEMPLE AND MUSEUM
288 South Bridge Road
Singapore 058840
Tel: 6220 0220
www.btrts.org.sg

__ 5 CHEN'S COLLECTIONS
36 Pagoda Street
Singapore 059195
Tel: 6226 6636

__ 6 CHINATOWN HERITAGE
CENTRE
48 Pagoda Street
Singapore 059207
Tel: 6338 6877
www.chinatownheritagecentre.sg

__ 7 CHINATOWN COMPLEX
Block 335 Smith Street
Chinatown Complex
Singapore 050335

__ 8 CHINESE OPERA TEAHOUSE
5 Smith Street, Singapore 058919
Tel: 6323 4862
www.ctcopera.com.sg/
teahouse.html

__ 9 CUGINI TRATTORIA PIZZERIA
87 Club Street #01-01,
Singapore 069455
Tel: 6221 3791
www.cugini.com.sg

__ 10 FIORE DORATO
48 Club Street, Singapore 069425
Tel: 6538 7227
www.fioredorato.com.sg

__ 11 FUK TAK CHI MUSEUM
76 Telok Ayer Street #01-01
Far East Square, Singapore 048464
Tel: 6532 7868
www.museums.com.sg/fu-tak-chi-museum/

__ 12 K KI /
THE LITTLE DRÖM STORE
7 Ann Siang Hill, Singapore 069791
Tel: 6225 6650 (K Ki)
Tel: 6225 5541 (The Little Dröm Store)
www.kki-sweets.com
thelittledromstore.com

___ 13 LAU PA SAT FESTIVAL MARKET
18 Raffles Quay
Singapore 048582
Tel: 6220 2138
www.laupasat.biz

___ 14 MING FANG ANTIQUE HOUSE
274 South Bridge Road
Singapore 058823
Tel: 6224 3788

___ 15 ODDS 'N' COLLECTABLES
128 Telok Ayer Street
Singapore 068597
Tel: 6323 0043

___ 16 RED DOT DESIGN MUSEUM
28 Maxwell Road
red dot Traffic
Singapore 069120
Tel: 6534 7001
www.reddottraffic.com

___ 17 RED STAR RESTAURANT
Blk 54 Chin Swee Road
#07-23
Singapore 160054
Tel: 6532 5266

___ 18 SINGAPORE GENERAL
HOSPITAL MUSEUM
Singapore General Hospital
Bowyer Block Clock Tower
11 Third Hospital Avenue
Singapore 168751
Tel: 6326 5294
www.sgh.com.sg

___ 19 SRI MARIAMMAN TEMPLE
244 South Bridge Road
Singapore 058793
Tel: 6223 4064

___ 20 STYLE:NORDIC
39 Ann Siang Road
Singapore 069716
Tel: 6423 9114
www.stylenordic.com

___ 21 THE ASYLUM SHOP
22 Ann Siang Road, Singapore 069702
www.theasylum.com.sg

___ 22 THE CLUB
28 Ann Siang Road, Singapore 069708
Tel: 6808 2188
www.theclub.com.sg

___ 23 TONG HENG CONFECTIONERY
285 South Bridge Road
Singapore 058833
Tel: 6223 3649, 6223 0398

___ 24 VIEW POINT TRADING
& COLLECTIBLES
18 Cross Street
#02-09, China Square Central
Singapore 048423
Tel: 6327 8063
www.viewpointtrading.com.sg

___ 25 WOODS IN THE BOOKS
58 Club Street, Singapore 069433
Tel: 6222 9980
www.woodsinthebooks.sg

037

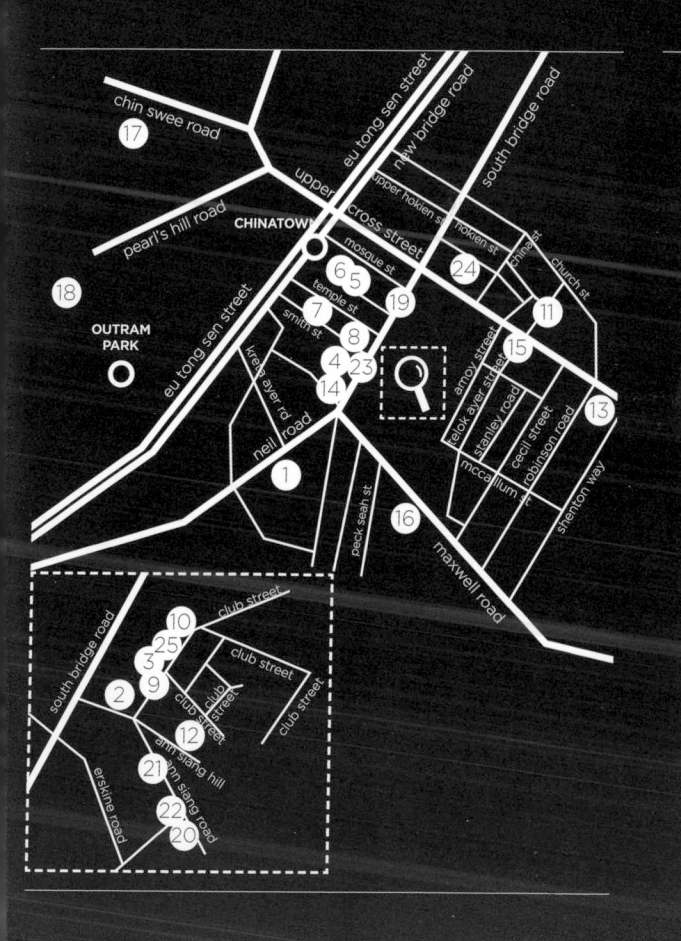

ENJOY TRADITIONAL CHINESE PASTRIES AT TONG HENG CONFECTIONERY

For some of the best traditional Chinese pastries in town, Tong Heng Confectionery has been around since the swinging 1920s and has never lost its magic touch. Still going strong along Chinatown's South Bridge Road, Tong Heng is where locals head for pastries during Chinese New Year, weddings and baby showers.

Don't resist the inviting aroma that is Tong Heng's tell-tale sign of its top-rate pastries. This humble store arguably serves some of the best egg tarts around. You'll soon be having warm memories of the melt-in-your-mouth egg custard paired with the perfectly-flaky pastry. The array of treats are on display for your choosing, including the unique spicy and sweet curry puffs; *char siew sao**, a golden-baked pastry with pork filling; *lao puo bing**, an old favorite known as wife's biscuit; and the fluffy egg cakes. Purchase at least five items and you'll get them packed in a good ol' traditional cardboard box.

DID YOU

Try Tong Heng's perfectly flaky egg tarts?

Take home five pastries in a festive cardboard box?

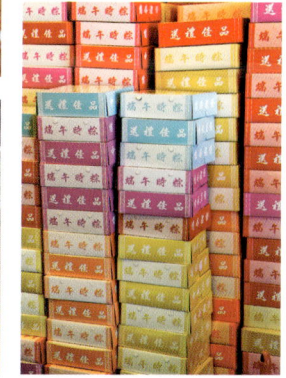

ENJOY TRADITIONAL CHINESE PASTRIES AT TONG HENG CONFECTIONERY

DISCOVER SINGAPORE'S FIRST STREET MUSEUM, FUK TAK CHI MUSEUM

This was the place where early Chinese immigrants would come upon arriving in Singapore. The reason: to offer thanksgiving for a safe passage to Fuk Tak Chi's patron deity, the earth god.

Gone are the coolies, the *Hakka**and *Cantonese** clan associations, the worshippers burning incense, and the nearby shoreline. Today, Fuk Tak Chi Museum is Singapore's first street museum surrounded by modern shopping and office complexes. A nostalgic gateway between Telok Ayer Street and Far East Square Mall, a visit to the Fuk Tak Chi Museum is akin to stepping into another world.

The museum has been carefully restored, retaining the original structure first built in 1825. Similar to a traditional Chinese magistrate court, the entrance is grand and imposing. Step inside to find a small courtyard, a shrine and a fascinating miniature of street life just half a century ago, a testament to the staggering changes the Fuk Tak Chi Museum has witnessed over the past century.

DID YOU

Admire miniature scenes of old Telok Ayer Street?

Snap a photo of old Chinatown artefacts?

DISCOVER SINGAPORE'S FIRST STREET MUSEUM, FUK TAK CHI MUSEUM

CHINATOWN

042

1. View Point Trading & Collectibles 2. Ming Fang Antique House 3. Chen's Collections 4. Odds 'N' Collectables

GO HUNTING FOR COLLECTIBLES

DID YOU

See everything from 1950s Singapore posters, precious Chinese artefacts and vintage drink bottles?

Chinatown is chock-a block with the typical souvenir store, but for the eclectic, the unusual, the artistic and the precious, Chinatown offers you its own little spots. Step headlong into...

... Odds 'N' Collectables, a ramshackle store spilling over with local collectibles. Not for the faint-hearted, wrestle though this untamed trove of items, including 1950s ads and posters, birdcages, cups, car plates and any artefact imaginable. A more Oriental experience, you ask — well, you might like...

... Ming Fang Antique House for its Chinese artefacts including Buddha statues, jade items and even Mao statues. Chen's Collections along souvenir-saturated Pagoda Street is a haunt for the true collector. Hunt down the precious figurines, wood or porcelain item here. For vintage curios, tarry down to...

.... View Point Trading & Collectibles at China Square Central. Patronised by many a celebrity, the store's choice collectibles are easy takeaways, including old records, cameras, drink paraphernalia, posters, suitcases and ashtrays.

WANDER ANN SIANG ROAD AND CLUB STREET

DID YOU

Poke your head inside a cool boutique or bookstore?

It's one way down and barely a breath pause along the lovely stretch that is Ang Siang Road and Club Street. Here's why this area has been such a draw for the designer and arty types...

Start off at The Club, a white-washed boutique hotel with a fine sky bar. Style:Nordic offers edgy Scandinavian labels, while The Asylum Shop, a fashionable retail store run by one of Singapore's top creative directors, rules the street. K Ki + The Little Dröm Store just off the main road offers pretty Japanese desserts and a wonderland of colourful knick knacks.

At the intersection of Ann Siang Road and Club Street, Beaujolais Wine Bar is the spot to savour the street's atmosphere. Head for some Southern Italian cuisine at this quaint joint, Cugini Trattoria Pizzeria. Literary buffs rejoice: you've arrived at Books Actually and Polymath & Crust, three stories that will satiate your book fetish; Woods in the Books completes the afternoon with a wide selection of picture books. Round off your afternoon with one of Singapore's best florists admiring exquisite blooms at Fiore Dorato.

1

1. Books Actually
2. K Ki + The Little Dröm Store
3. Fiore Dorato 4. Style:Nordic
5. Woods in the Books

WANDER ANN SIANG ROAD AND CLUB STREET

045

WATCH CHINESE OPERA AT THE CHINESE OPERA TEAHOUSE

DID YOU

Tuck into a Chinese set dinner while watching opera?

Take a photo with an opera singer?

Home to afternoon karaoke sessions, come Friday and Saturday evenings and the Chinese Opera Teahouse brings on the bright lights and stage action. Stealing the show at this small, quaint teahouse managed by the Chinese Theatre Circle is a Chinese opera performance where you'll get to be up close and personal with the singers.

Your evening begins with a Chinese dinner set, brewed tea and dessert in an intimate, long room with furnishings similar to typical teahouses. The room barely sits more than 20 people; you'll start feeling the atmosphere when show time hits at 8pm, and the opera singers put on a colourful demonstration and opera performance on the small stage (English subtitles included). End the night with a spot of photo-taking all for S$35. Reservations are needed, so you'll need to contact ctopera@yahoo.com or ring (+65) 6323 4862.

WATCH CHINESE OPERA AT THE CHINESE OPERA TEAHOUSE

047

DID YOU

Witness true-to-life living conditions in old Chinatown?

Have a drink at Chinatown Heritage Centre's brightly hued *kopi tiam**?

UNRAVEL CHINATOWN'S HISTORY AT THE CHINATOWN HERITAGE CENTRE

Singapore's Chinese forefathers took a treacherous trip across the seas to pursue a better life — the traces of these original immigrants are imprinted everywhere in Chinatown. While today, one can only behold the modern face of this historic enclave, the Chinatown Heritage Centre documents an important slice of history for 21st century visitors.

A trip here is surely a nostalgic and revealing insight into Singapore's roots. Housed in three shop houses, the Chinatown Heritage Centre offers visitors an honest, true-to-life recreation of living conditions in the 1950s. Be witness to those times, as immigrants struggled through squalid living conditions and vice, while forming clan associations and celebrating traditional festivals to foster a sense of community in a foreign land. It's enough to make you feel the heartache and sweat of the people who built this country from the ground. Be transported back to modern Chinatown and marvel the transformation at the Chinatown Heritage Centre's brightly hued *kopi tiam** on the ground level.

THINK DESIGN AT THE RED DOT DESIGN MUSEUM

DID YOU

Discover award-wining product designs from the red dot design awards?

Pick up drool-worthy items at the red dot design shop?

Just in case you need an introduction into the brave new world of contemporary design, here's a 101: the red dot design awards is one of the most prestigious awards in the design industry, conferred to only the best and brightest. Here at Singapore's red dot design museum (the sister museum of the famous red dot museum in Germany), you'll find the award-winning works of past winners in the product design category.

Housed in the red dot traffic building, simply unmistakable for its fire-engine red façade, the building is a beacon for the city's growing interest in design. And unlike other museums, the design works on exhibition speak not to the past, but the future. Head here to get stimulated by the ideas and innovations from product prototypes imagining new possibilities in everyday living. Design geeks, rejoice — get your fix for drool-worthy design items at the red dot design shop on the ground level.

THINK DESIGN AT THE RED DOT DESIGN MUSEUM

DID YOU

Catch a glimpse of the Buddha tooth relic in the golden inner chamber?

DISCOVER THE BUDDHA TOOTH RELIC TEMPLE AND MUSEUM

This temple in the heart of Chinatown cost a staggering S$75 million to lease, construct and fill with artefacts. Be a witness to the Buddha Tooth Relic Temple and Museum's grand Mandala-inspired architecture and interior décor based on the art of the Tang Dynasty.

Devotees say the Buddha Tooth Relic Temple and Museum houses a sacred item, a relic known to be the tooth of the Buddha. This is the temple's main highlight and namesake; on the fourth floor, you'll discover a 3.6-metre-high, 426-kilogrammes-heavy gold stupa housing the relic (around half the gold was donated by devotees). You can only view the inner chamber twice a day so be sure to check out the times.

Wander around the temple's four floors and visit a Buddhist Cultural Museum, a relic chamber, an ancestral memorial hall, pagodas on the roof and the Lotus Heart teahouse serving vegetarian fare.

VISIT THE
SRI MARIAMMAN TEMPLE

Visit Singapore's oldest temple after its most recent facelift in 2010. The restoration reportedly cost S$4 million where Indian artists were brought in to restore the vivid colours of 21 granite gods and goddesses of the temple.

The temple is dedicated to the goddess Sri Mariamman, whom South Indian Hindus revere for her protection from calamity and disease. You'll recognise the temple along South Bridge Road by its awe-inspiring *gopuram** with sculptures of gods in six tiers and life-sized statues of scared cows sitting atop the walls.

Prayers and rituals are conducted daily. Entrance here is free, though you have to pay a small fee for photo and video-taking.

VISIT THE SRI MARIAMMAN TEMPLE

DID YOU

Admire Sri Mariamman Temple's awe-inspiring *gopuram**?

DISCOVER PERANAKAN HERITAGE AT THE BABA HOUSE

Who are the Peranakans? Descendents of Chinese immigrants who came to Malaya (today's Malaysia and Singapore), this group gradually evolved a unique culture blending indigenous Malay customs with Chinese traditions.

The Baba House provides a window into their world circa 1928, when Peranakan traditions were much alive here. You'll find 60 to 70 percent of the furniture, including the ancestral shrine and wedding beds, intact from the home's original owners, the Wee family. In its heyday, up to three generations of the Wee family lived under its roofs.

Managed by the National University of Singapore (NUS) Museum and the NUS Centre for the Arts, discover the carefully restored treasures of this disappearing culture. The first two floors are a true-to-life reconstruction of a Peranakan home, where you'll be privy to antiques, furnishings, the social customs and cultural motifs of the Pernakans. The third level showcases exhibitions of Peranakan culture.

Visits are by appointment only. For enquiries, contact (+65) 6227 5731 or babahouse@nus.edu.sg.

DID YOU

Learn to tell the difference between a *baba** and a *bibik**?

Discover the social customs and cultural motifs of the Peranakans?

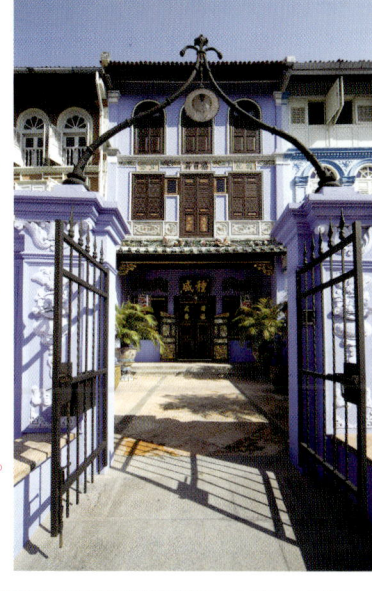

DISCOVER PERANAKAN HERITAGE AT THE BABA HOUSE

CATCH WET MARKET SCENES ON SMITH STREET

Wet markets are a bona fide Singaporean institution. Welcome to the Garden City, a little less manicured, a little less clean. Be warned about the nasty smell of raw food, but there's no place better to watch locals engage in a no-holds-barred haggling for daily food items.

Head to Chinatown Complex at Smith Street for colourful wet market scenes at the building's basement. A good pair of shoes is mandatory (the floors are as slippery as they come); bring small change if you like to shop, and an appetite for the raucous sights and sounds.

Come before noon (early morning is best) when all the live stock is fresh and lined up for the taking. Wander along the open-air poultry, fish and vegetable stores; the hawkers haggle, slice and pack with seasoned finesse. The housewives and grannies are here for the freshest and cheapest — and they'll jostle their way through any crowd. Take heart, brave traveller — if it all gets too much, the hawker centre above offers a respite.

DID YOU

Come to the wet market before noon to catch hawkers in action?

CATCH WET MARKET SCENES ON SMITH STREET

DID YOU

Order ten sticks of chicken, beef or mutton *satay**?

Watch the hawkers fan the *satay** sticks?

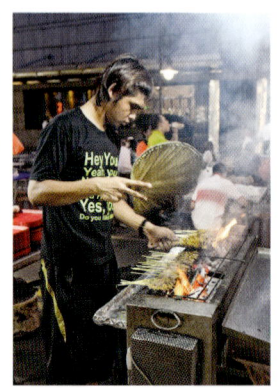

FEAST ON LOCAL FAVOURITE, SATAY, AT LAU PA SAT

Come evening, and this street next to Lau Pa Sat Festival Market is where *satay** street hawkers come out in full force. Unlike the more civilised hawkers inside the market, these hawkers do it the old-school way, fanning sticks of marinated meat on a grill in pushcarts. Head here after 6pm to catch these hawkers in action.

These *satay** sticks are as good they come. Tuck into the local flavours with sweet and spicy peanut sauce, and *lontong** wrapped in banana leaves. Your challenge for the night would be to decide which vendor to patronise as the enthusiastic storeowners will certainly jostle for your business. Order at least ten sticks to have your fill, and ask for the usual favourites such as chicken, beef and mutton *satay**.

Simply put, the atmosphere is fantastic, what with *satay** in hand and dining *al fresco* in a night market atmosphere. Oh, and don't forget your Tiger beer.

DISCOVER THE SINGAPORE GENERAL HOSPITAL MUSEUM

DID YOU

Get a glimpse of Singapore General Hospital's history during the Second World War?

With Singapore's rising reputation as a medical tourism hub, the Singapore General Hospital (SGH) Museum will show you a thing or two about the medical milestones this nation has undergone.

Just a little off Chinatown, closer to Pearl's Hill, the SGH Museum is housed in the Bower Block. The interesting bits at this museum are purely historical. Imagine the SGH as a wooden shed in 1821: see first hand the dark times during the Japanese Occupation from 1942 to 1945, where the hospital staff attended to the many war victims.

Known as the People's Hospital, the development of SGH's facilities and medical specialties has had a lasting impact on Singaporeans. You'll get to watch interviews with past doctors and SGH luminaries who will unravel the rise of this local medical institution.

DISCOVER THE SINGAPORE GENERAL HOSPITAL MUSEUM

DID YOU

Hustle waitresses to get a plate of your favourite *dim sum** off a trolley cart?

HAVE TRADITIONAL DIM SUM AT RED STAR RESTAURANT

This place doesn't take reservations so queue up on a Sunday morning to see what the fuss is all about.

Red Star Restaurant has long been a stalwart for Cantonese *dim sum** in Singapore. The main draw? Waitresses pushing trolley carts serving piping-hot *dim sum** Hong-Kong style. For the uninitiated, this is both a delightful culinary experience, as well as a (good) chance to preview what you're eating before you order it. A whopping 90 types of *dim sum** on the menu might leave you spoilt for choice. Try popular favourites as *cheong fun**, *chaw siew sao**, fried prawn rolls, century egg congee and *har-gau**.

Food critics from all walks will have their say on the culinary rise and fall of this restaurant, but one thing's undeniable – the nostalgic atmosphere, à la a typical Chinese wedding banquet circa 1980, will make this an experience to savour.

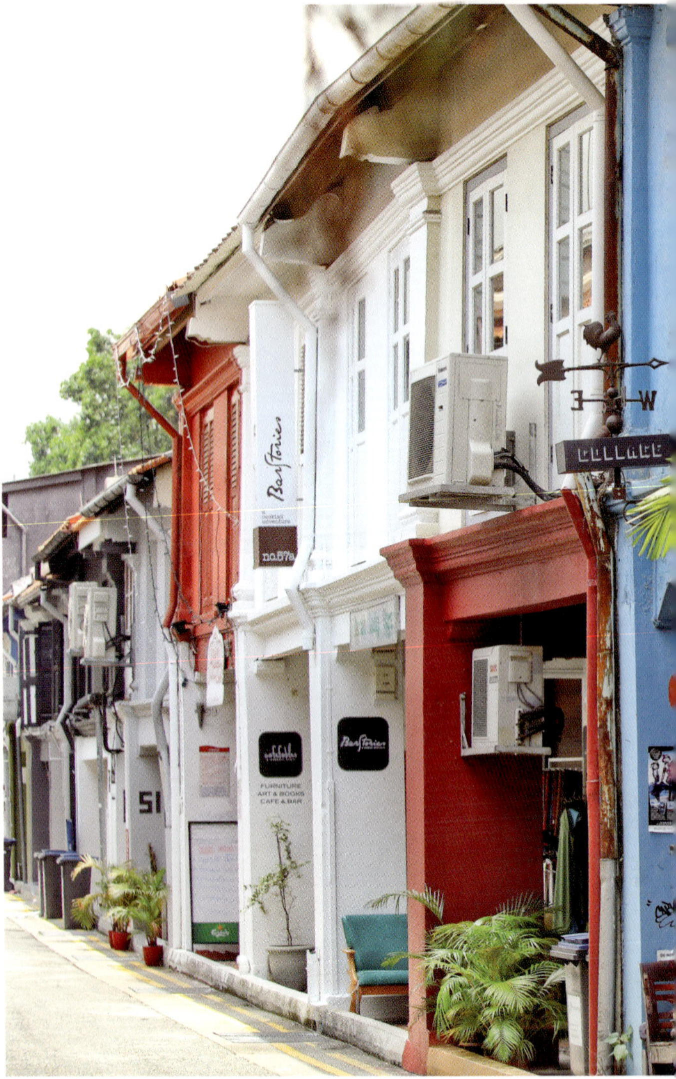
FURNITURE
ART & BOOKS
CAFE & BAR
51

ARAB STREET / BUGIS

Bugis was once known as Boogie Street in the swinging 1950s when transgendered ran a roaring sex trade. Just two-steps away, Kampong Glam used to be a fishing village by the Rochor River; today, the area exudes a strong Malay-Arab flavour passed down from colonial days when the British designated the area to the Malays, Arabs and Bugis (an ethnic group from South Sulawesi).

Kampong Glam and Bugis today aren't snooty neighbourhoods – so you can loosen up and soak in the area's street-level buzz. Exiting from Bugis train station, you're bound to hit the shopping malls, Bugis Junction and Illuma, a haunt for teeny-boppers (enter cutesy items and cheap eats). But venture out to meet the area's denizens: from young creatives hanging out after classes, to grungy individuals who man their boutiques, food vendors, older ladies shopping for textiles, and an eclectic crowd seeking Middle-Eastern cuisine.

Bugis and Kampong Glam extend all the way from Middle Road to Jalan Sultan. The surrounding lanes around the Bugis train station are bustling with street bazaars and food joints, so you'll be spoilt for choice when peckish. Around Kampong Glam's Arab Street is where a palpable Malay-Arab influence hangs in the air – watch out for Arab Street's golden landmark - Singapore's oldest mosque, the Sultan Mosque. Rummage through the textiles, handicrafts, *batik*, souvenirs, and off-kilter stores along the streets of Bussorah, Muscat, Baghdad, Haji Lane and Bali Lane. We also recommend spending heady evenings reveling in the area's Middle-Eastern vibe.

THE SPOTS

___ 1 ALTAZZAG EGYPTIAN RESTAURANT
24 Haji Lane, Singapore 189217
Tel: 6295 5024

___ 2 AMBROSIA, THE MEDITERRANEAN RESTAURANT
19 Baghdad Street, Singapore 199658
Tel: 6292 7313
www.ambrosiacafesingapore.com

___ 3 BLACKMARKET
19 Jalan Pisang, Singapore 199084
Tel: 6296 8512
www.theblackmarket.sg

___ 4 BLU JAZ CAFÉ
11 Bali Lane, Singapore 189848
Tel: 6292 3800
www.blujaz.net

___ 5 BUGIS VILLAGE STREET BAZAAR
Opposite Bugis Junction
Shopping Mall
www.bugis-street.com

___ 6 CAFÉ LE CAIRE
39 Arab Street, Singapore 199736
Tel: 6292 0979
www.cafelecaire.com

___ 7 FIKA SWEDISH CAFÉ AND BISTRO
257 Beach Road
Singapore 199539
Tel: 6396 9096
www.fikacafe.com

___ 8 JAMAL KAZURA AROMATICS
21 Bussorah Street
Singapore 199439
Tel: 6293 3320

___ 9 KNOW IT NOTHING
51 Haji Lane
Singapore 189244
Tel: 6392 5475
www.knowitnothing.com

___ 10 LOFT & PUBLIC
16A Haji Lane, Singapore 189209
Tel: 6297 0169
loft.com.sg

___ 11 MALAY HERITAGE CENTRE
85 Sultan Gate
Singapore 198501
Tel: 6391 0450
www.malayheritage.org.sg

___ 12 MINT MUSEUM OF TOYS
26 Seah Street, Singapore 188382
Tel: 6339 0660
www.emint.com

___ 13 PLUCK
31/33 Haji Lane, Singapore 189226
Tel: 6396 4048
www.pluck.com.sg

___ 14 NATIONAL LIBRARY SINGAPORE
100 Victoria Street, Singapore 188064
Tel: 6332 3255
www.nl.sg

___ 15 RATTAN HANDICRAFT
58 Arab Street
Singapore 199755

___ 16 SOON LEE
73 Haji Lane
Singapore 189266
www.ishopsoonlee.blogspot.com

___ 17 STRAITS RECORDS
49 Haji Lane
Singapore 189242
www.myspace.com/straitsrecords

___ 18 TAWAKAL ORIENTAL CARPETS
50 Arab Street, Singapore 199747
Tel: 6292 2340

___ 19 TOKO ALJUNIED
95 Arab Street
Singapore 199791
Tel: 6294 6897

___ 20 THE BLOG SHOP
35 Haji Lane
Singapore 189228
Tel: 6396 6170
theblogshop.sg

___ 21 ZAM ZAM
697 North Bridge Road
Singapore 198675
Tel: 6298 6320

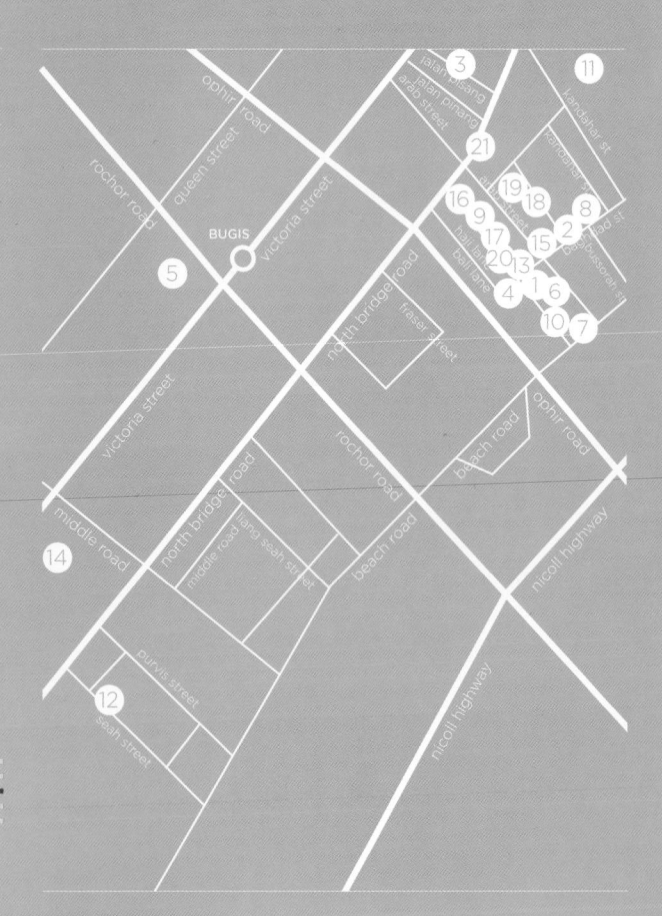

ARAB STREET/BUGIS

PICK UP COOL THREADS AT BLACKMARKET

DID YOU

Get up to speed with the movers and shakers of the Singapore fashion scene?

Fashion goes local at cooler-than-cool multi-label store Blackmarket. Edgy is the name of the game here – so put on some spunk and get ready to get hip from head to toe.

The store throbs with the latest collections from the movers and shakers of the Singaporean street fashion circles. More than 32 local labels gather here, from punk-chic label FrüFrü & Tigerlily, to the sculptured dresses of Yumumu, and the mysterious threads of menswear label Cloak & Dagger.

Blackmarket naturally also shows it love for cult designers, both regional and international. Part of the eclectic mix includes Australian androgynous jewellery line Does Not Equal, and Indonesian label Nikicio. Not forgetting international cult faves like Juliette Has A Gun fragrances, Vonzipper sunglasses, and Nooka watches. Don't step out without your shades.

LOOK UP INDEPENDENT BOUTIQUES AT HAJI LANE

Young hearts, run free... along Haji Lane. This may look like a tiny little back alley, but come closer to unravel why this cluster of quirky retail stores and independent boutiques are such a magnet for young creative types.

Turn up after 1pm from Monday to Saturdays to find the stores open and in full swing. Resident style haven Soon Lee is good for sassy dresses and bags; while online bloggers make their presence felt at The Blog Shop where they hawk their best stuff in the real world.

Pick up nifty carriers for your laptop with Fabrix Cases at Loft & Public. Know It Nothing celebrates craftsmanship for men with taste – with shirts, suits and designer glasses that are spiffy to a T. Finally, settle down for a scoop of ice cream at Pluck along with their sumptuous furnishings and accessories.

075

LOOK UP INDEPENDENT BOUTIQUES AT HAJI LANE

RECOMMENDED FOR

Those who seek alternative fashion with a youthful edge.

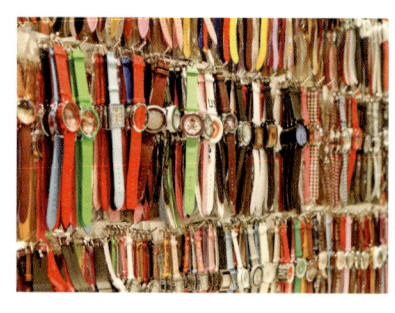

DID YOU

Walk the street bazaar from Victoria Street to Queen Street?

GO STREET SHOPPING AT BUGIS VILLAGE STREET BAZAAR

Transvestites brought in the crowds with cabaret performances in the 1950s, but Bugis Village has since been turned into Singapore's largest street bazaar.

This ongoing *pasar malam** at Bugis Village is your best bet for a taste of Singaporean street shopping. Nestled in the area opposite shopping mall Bugis Junction, cross the street to head smack into the bazaar which stretches from Victoria Street all the way to Queen Street.

Expect cheap prices, and an eclectic mix of souvenirs, watches, street wear, bags and DVDs while you rub shoulders with the crowd. No bazaar outing will be complete without some food, so be sure to check out the hawker stores and fruit juice stands.

RELIVE CHILDHOOD MEMORIES AT THE MINT MUSEUM OF TOYS

If you've ever regretted throwing away those old Barbie Dolls and GI Joes, there's a pretty good chance you'll see them again at Mint Museum of Toys.

Nope, these toys are not for sale (the collection is worth an estimated whopping S$5 million) but a S$15 dollar ticket will get you in to view a collection of 50,000 toys, from over 40 countries, whose lineage stretches over a century.

Impressive numbers aside, more impressive is how one man – engineering consultant Chang Yang Fa – amassed the collection over a 30-year period. This private museum was set up in the hope of igniting that Moment of Imagination and Nostalgia with Toys (read: Mint). Go gaga over vintage Marvel heroes and the Disney pantheon, nostalgic Betty Boop, Tintin and Popeye toys, and marvel rare pieces miraculously culled from the 1800s.

DID YOU

Go gaga over Marvel Heroes, Betty Boop, Tintin and Popeye Toys?

GET YOUR UNDERGROUND MUSIC FIX AT STRAITS RECORDS

DID YOU

Spin a track of Jamaican reggae, hardcore punk or bands from Indonesia and Malaysia?

Call them the Kampong Glam Warriors or Singapore's Soul of the Underground – whatever it is, Straits Records is a veritable local music institution.

This independent music store has been flying the flag for music subculture with undying fervour since 1999. From its red-hot logo with punching fists to shop owner's Wan Vegan's striking beard and long locks, everything about Straits Records says forget the naysayers, let's keep the underground music scene alive.

The store stocks a discerning selection of Jamaican reggae, hardcore punk, to hip hop, alternative and bands from Indonesia and Malaysia. This is the place where local bands first put out their demos, where you'll find a sounding board for up-and coming musicians. Stick your head in here and you might just find tickets for a great gig that's coming to town.

BIBLIOPHILES, SEEK RELIEF AT THE NATIONAL LIBRARY BUILDING

Smack in the middle of the Bugis area, the sixteen-storey-tall National Library Building beckons with its bountiful books, and as a spot to rest your feet and catch a quiet moment.

The building is popular with locals for its accessible location and plentiful seating. At the building's basement is the Central Lending Library. Here's where you'll find people picking up the daily newspapers and magazines, to university students mugging at quiet corners. If you're up for a read, there's a section dedicated to local literature, and the latest library recommendations on display.

From the 7th to 13th floors, find the Lee Kong Chian Reference Library. The books aren't allowed out of the premises, and you could hear a pin drop here as handphones are to be strictly switched to silent mode. But for serious readers, there are laudable collections in the business, arts, and Asia-related fields.

DID YOU

Check out the National Library's laudable collections in business, arts and Asia-related fields?

PUFF THE MAGIC DRAGON: SHISHA

DID YOU

Soak in Arab Street's down tempo vibe while puffing shisha in cosy niches?

What do you do after a platter of shish kebab and saffron rice? Here's an idea: when in Arab Street, act like an Arabian and smoke Shisha.

Shisha in Singapore is similar to its global counterparts: coals burn out flavoured tobacco, the smoke passes through a water pipe, out of mouthpieces and into the lungs.

The difference lies in *where*.

Most restaurants such as Ambrosia, the Mediterranean Restaurant and Café Le Caire let you dine and puff away in cosy niches along the pavements surrounded by lamps pieced together from mosaic tiles and lovely plush carpets. All the better for you to soak in Arab Street's down tempo vibe, whilst shooting the breeze – or in this case, flavoured smoke – with friends.

DID YOU

Embrace ethnic finds such as Thai silks, *batik* shirts, and Oriental carpets?

SHOPAHOLICS, BUY ETHNIC CURIOS FROM ARAB STREET

The shopping's great at Arab Street... if you're not looking for a designer fashionista outfit (that's what Orchard Road's for). As once upon a Rafflesian era, the area imported whatever the local Muslim community needed.

This tradition remains and it's quite visible in Kampong Glam's wares of Arabian/Muslim origin around Arab Street.

There are intricately woven carpets (check out Tawakal Oriental Carpets); a bewildering array of fabrics like Thai silks, glittery sequins, or French lace (anywhere along Arab Street); wicker chairs, baskets and cutesy rattan handicrafts (head to Rattan Handicraft); non-alcholic perfumes (make a beeline for Jamal Kazura Aromatics) that are custom-crafted to the wearer; and *batik** shirts as well as diaphanous *sarong kebaya** (look for Toko Aljunied).

1,7. Rattan Handicraft 2. Jamal Kazura Aromatics 3,6. Toko Aljunied 4,5. Tawakal Oriental Carpets

EAT YOUR WAY AROUND THE WORLD... AROUND ARAB STREET

DID YOU

Take your pick of meats from *murtabak**, kebabs, Swedish-style meatballs or *bak kut teh**?

It's a cinch to get Mediterranean and Arabian cuisines around Arab Street. But did you know the area is also home to the world's cuisines?

There's great *briyanis** and fluffed-up *murtabak** at Zam Zam for a gastronomic trip to the Indian sub-continent. The Middle Eastern nations are best experienced with hummus, pita and kebabs at Altazzag Egyptian Restaurant whilst sitting on carpets along Haji Lane's *five-foot ways**.

The western hemisphere is represented by the ever-popular Blu Jaz Café with its quirky décor, kick-ass jazz performances and big ol' burgers. Or just head around the corner to Fika Swedish Cafe and Bistro for Swedish-style meatballs and potatoes... Halal of course.

Finally, Orientalists should trawl Beach Road for their many steamboat restaurants and *Klang**-styled herbal *bak kut teh**.

1. Al-Tazzag 2. Fika
3. Zam Zam 4. Blu Jaz Café

ARAB STREET/BUGIS

VISIT A SLICE OF HISTORY AT THE MALAY HERITAGE CENTRE

RECOMMENDED FOR

Discovering all things to know about Singapore's Malay Community

What are we if we don't know our roots?

We'd be like driftwood out at sea.

That's why the Malay Heritage Centre is important to Singaporeans. This stone and burnished wood encyclopedic location contains all things to know about Singapore's Malays, especially since the area was the original settlement for the Malays assigned by the British during the colonial era.

Housed within the old Istana Kampong Gelam, the Malay Heritage Centre has nine galleries that chronologically showcase the story of Singapore's Malays. We particularly like Gallery Six as it features the golden age of Malay entertainment in the region (think iconic director and musician: P. Ramlee.).

The centre's grounds are also great for a stroll in the evening, so end your visit at the museum around 6pm. Also, if you happen to visit during the month of Ramadan, walk around the streets around the compound, as they are turned into a bustling market in the evenings.

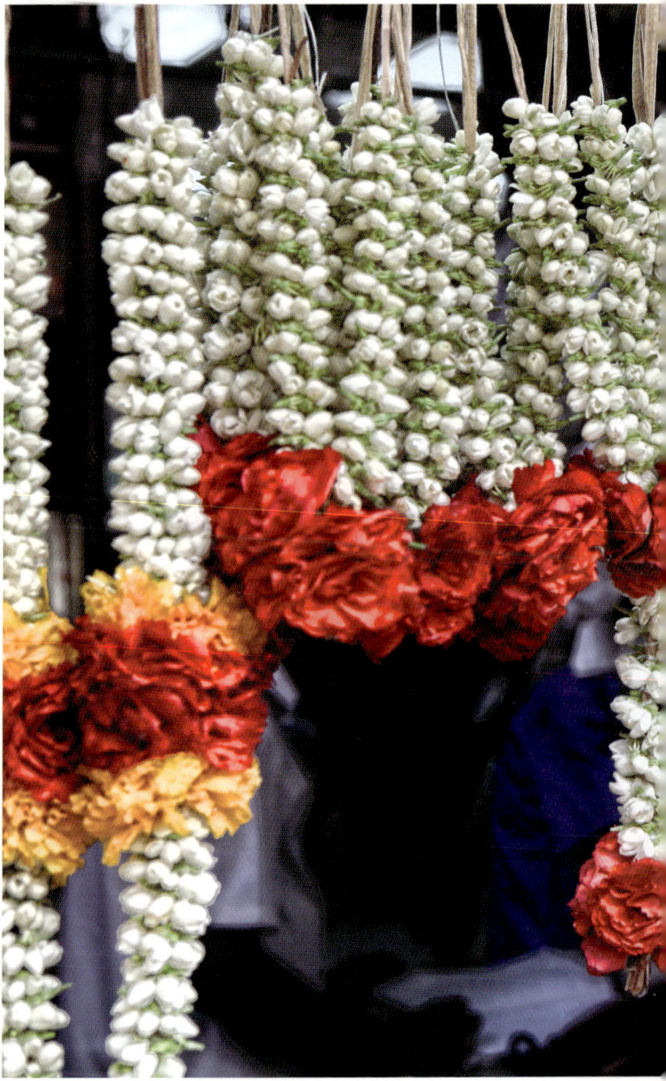

LITTLE INDIA

Get under the skin of Singapore's Little India to find an area steaming and teeming with life. From the colourful and cultural temples and Indian stores, to the rambunctious streets and (sometimes) shady alleyways, Little India has it all.

The main streets running through Little India are Serangoon Road and Jalan Besar where stores blare the latest Bollywood ditties, while selling Indian sweets, gold bangles and spices. You'll find some of the street names strangely Western – Campbell Lane, Clive Street, Dickson Road – a throwback to the early 1800s when this place was mostly an European residential area.

The attractions of Little India are best had on foot, so take off into the little back lanes to catch a glimpse of the area's many faces. Cultural sights abound, from colourful flower garlands, the ladies in their *saris** and the tempting array of curry, *dahl**, *papadam** and *thosai** at every turn. On Cuff Street, find one of the last spice-grinding stores in town. Savour market scenes on Buffalo Road, or admire portraits of Hindu deities at the galleries on Kerbau Road. Around Dunlop Street, Prince of Wales Backpackers Pub has become a haunt for live music gigs and a pint of beer for the backpacking crowd. Come here on a Sunday, and Little India is an absolute riot, where the whole community of foreign Indian nationals seem to converge.

THE SPOTS

__ 1 BANANA LEAF APOLO
56 Race Course Road
Singapore 218564
Tel: 6293 8682
www.thebananaleafapolo.com

__ 2 CHETTINADU NEW RESTAURANT
41 Chander Road, Singapore 219543
Tel: 6291 7161

__ 3 FOOD #03
107/109 Rowell Road
Post Museum
Singapore 208033
Tel: 6396 7980
www.food03.sg

__ 4 LAND TRANSPORT GALLERY
No. 1 Hampshire Road
Singapore 219428
Tel: 6396 2550
www.lta.gov.sg

__ 5 LITTLE INDIA ARCADE
48 Serangoon Road
Singapore 217959

__ 6 MUSTAFA CENRE
145 Syed Alwi Rd, Singapore 207704
Tel: 6295 5855
www.mustafa.com.sg

__ 7 NEW KAARAIKUDI BANANA LEAF RESTAURANT
131 Serangoon Road
Singapore 218036

__ 8 SRI VEERAMAKALIAMMAN TEMPLE
141 Serangoon Road
Singapore 218042
Tel: 6295 4538; 6293 4634
www.sriveeramakaliamman.com

__ 9 SUNGEI ROAD THIEVES MARKET
Around Sungei Rd

093

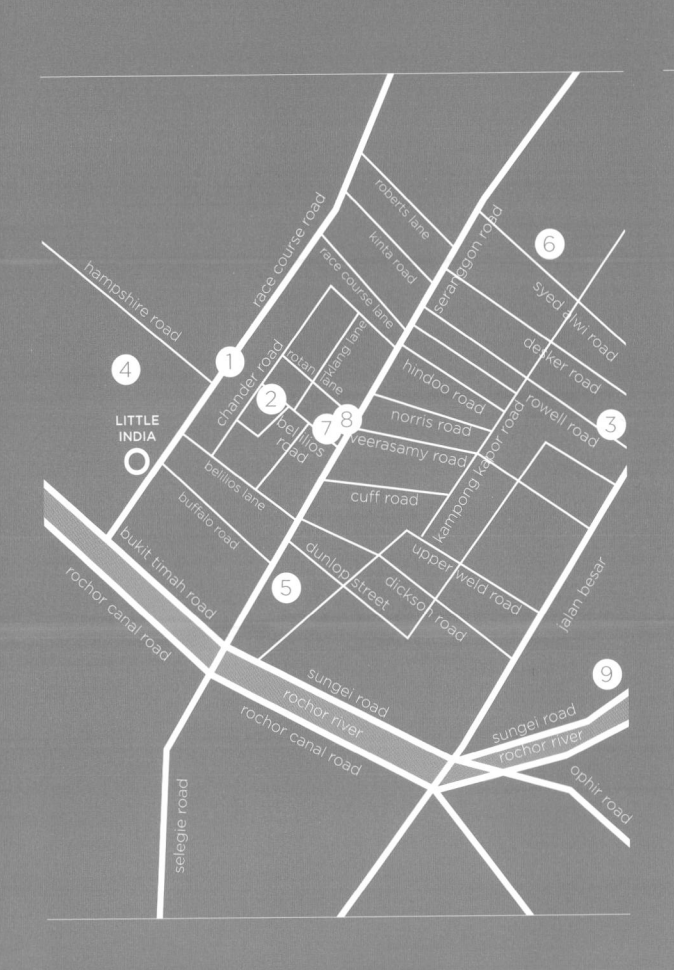

BURN THE MIDNIGHT OIL SHOPPING AT MUSTAFA CENTRE

Lucky for you midnight owls, Singapore doesn't get much shut-eye. Late-night supper joints are a staple here, but for those restless nights, look to Mustafa Centre, Singapore's only mall that stays open every day, all day.

It's not just the bargains here that makes Mutafa Centre so fascinating – it's the sheer variety of wares on display. Trawling through this 75,000 square feet, six-level shopping complex may be a mammoth task – especially with narrow lanes, and dizzying arrangements – but it's well worth the effort.

Where else can you pick up everything from electronics, home appliances, jewellery, textiles, clothes, cosmetics, fragrances, to DVDs at bargain prices? Or find in its departmental store food brands from nations such as Turkey and Iran along with an incomparable array of Indian spices? Just remember how to find your way home – you're unlikely to end up where you started.

DID YOU

Trawl through this 75,000 square feet mall for bargains in electronics, food stuffs and fragrances?

INDULGE IN A ROTI PRATA AND TEH TARIK

The Italians relish their black coffee, the English are big on beer... here in Singapore's Little India, we call our everyday simple pleasure *roti prata** and *teh tarik**.

And remember: half the fun comes from watching these treats being prepared. Catch the *roti prata** chef as he flips pieces of flour dough in the air, to serve you a flat, grilled pancake with curry (ask for the egg or onion version for extra oomph).

And while *teh** (tea) can be found island-wide, the *teh tarik** made here is probably the ultimate indulgence. Ask the drink maker to show you how he pours the tea between two cups. The result: an extra-frothy, extra-smooth blend of black tea flavoured with condensed milk, perfect for any afternoon break.

The good news: you can find these in almost any coffee shop in Little India, and they won't cost you more than two dollars.

DID YOU

Watch how *roti prata** and *teh tarik** are made?

GO VEGAN (AND DO GOOD) AT FOOD #03

It's incongruous that Food #03 – a social experiment/art project/vegan restaurant – resides in one of Little India's dodgiest streets. Think meat market, but clothed in *saris* and heavy makeup. Maybe that's why this quaint restaurant is entirely meatless in a bold statement on what goes on outside?

Regardless, it's a place to unleash your inner herbivore as their Tempeh Burger, Pu-er Tea Noodles, and Asparagus with Shitake Mushrooms pizza have garnered rave reviews from diners.

At the same time, learn to be more socially aware with Food #03's Save-the-Earth workshops, which might involve pounding vegetable scraps into garbage enzymes, or share your things and services at their Really Really Free Markets, well...for free.

HEAD HERE TO

Unleash your inner herbivore on Tempeh burgers and Shitake mushroom pizzas.

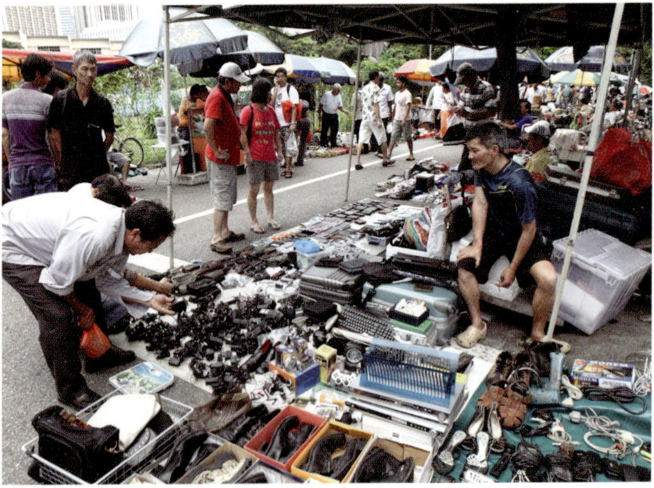

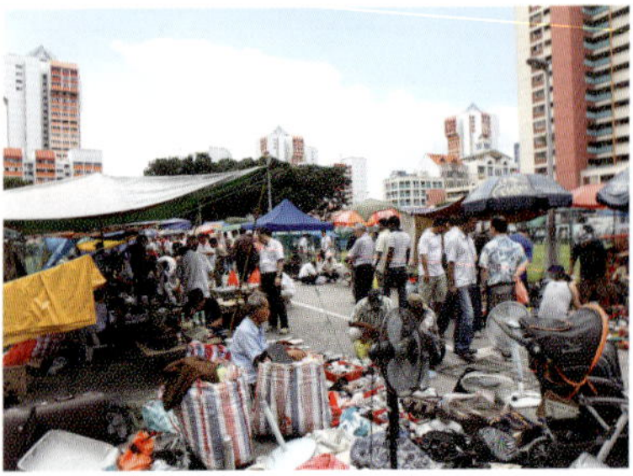

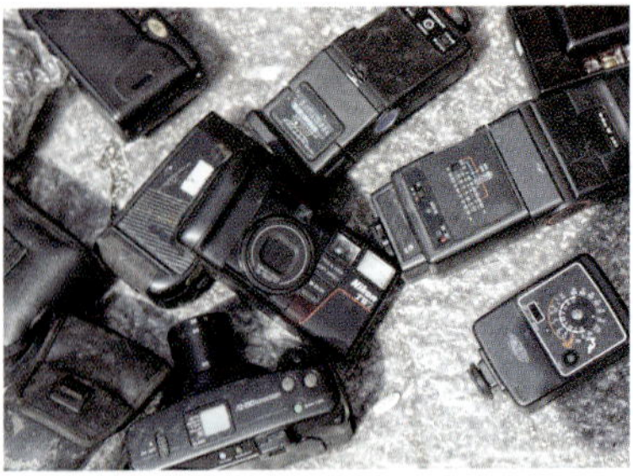

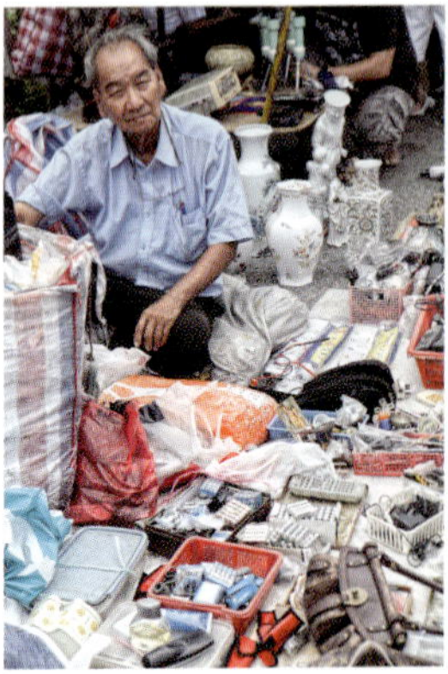

DIG FOR TREASURE AT SUNGEI ROAD THIEVES MARKET

WORTH A TRIP

To scavenge rare finds, from old banana notes from the Japanese Occupation to vintage cameras.

The Sungei Road Thieves Market may have shed its shady past as a hotspot for looted ware in the 1930s. But fast-forward to the 21st century and Singapore's oldest flea market still hawks scavenged second-hand items and random bric-a-brac (just don't ask where these items are from).

Located along the Rochor Canal, expect sun, sweat and lots of makeshift stores (read: spread out tarpaulin sheets with items stacked up for the taking). You'll find an older generation of street peddlers every day from 11am to 7pm.

But lest you think it's all trash and no treasure, look again. Enthusiasts will vouch that there are rare finds and old, nostalgic items galore, here for the taking. On offer may be banana notes from the Japanese Occupation, old movie posters from the 1930s, vintage lomography cameras, old records, and good ol' beverage memorabilia. And remember: haggling is mandatory.

VISIT THE
LAND TRANSPORT GALLERY

WORTH A VISIT

To discover the historical origins of Singapore's efficient transport system

Fast, efficient, and ever-evolving – Singapore's transport system is a source of national pride. But how did this island-nation go from rickety trishaws in the early 1900s to the high-tech trains and buses today?

Well, the Land Transport Gallery, dedicated to Singapore's transportation history, may give you some insight. The gallery's six zones are chronologically arranged, taking you from old traffic control measures in pre-independent Singapore to the nostalgic 70s and 80s when bus conductors punched bus tickets and gave exact change to passengers.

It's back to the future at the end of the gallery tour, with a futuristic peer into what Singapore's transportation landscape may be like come 2030. Admission to the Land Transport Gallery is free, but you'll have to book three days in advance for a one-hour tour. The gallery opens Tuesdays to Sundays at these tour times: 9am, 11am, 1pm and 3pm.

TO SHELTER! TO SHELTER! IN SRI VEERAMAKALIAMMAN TEMPLE

DID YOU

Enter the temple to admire the gate tower of Hindu deities?

Listen: "During World War 2, when there were air raids, many took refuge in the temple and were safe there. The temple and those within escaped the bombings unscathed."

Perhaps Kali, the chief deity of Sri Veeramakaliamman Temple, was looking out for her faithful in their time of need. That's not surprising as she is the destroyer of evil. Just enter the temple to see how a skull-garlanded Kali disembowelled her victims. Strangely enough, the images also include family moments with her sons: Ganesha and Murugan.

The temple has expanded to include 12 other deities such as the elephant-headed Lord Vinayagar. Check their website (www.sriveeramakaliamman.com) on the best methods and timings to pray to each deity.

PS: Look up when going under the gate tower. It's the best spot to view the many deities of the Hindu pantheon.

MIND YOUR LEAFWARE MANNERS! OR BANANA LEAVES AS PLATES

In India, banana leaves are commonly used as plates. They're easily available, big, and fragrant, which makes them perfect for containing food. All you have to do is just pile on the curries and rice, eat, and burn the plat...leaf. It's hygienic, environmentally-friendly, and strangely enough, eating food off a banana leaf just tastes better.

But what goes best on a banana leaf? Anything.

It could be Rava Onion *thosai** surrounded by slopping heaps of chutney, sambar and *dhal**. Or a mountain of *briyani** rice steeped with mutton and topped with a *papadum**. Or fluffy rice covered by your fancy of vegetables, meats and curries (we recommend the fish head curry).

And forget about the cutlery, instead eat with your hands, but remember always use the right hand. Learn your leafware manners at these choice restaurants: Banana Leaf Apolo; New Kaaraikudi Banana Leaf Restaurant; and Chettinadu New Restaurant.

YOU MIGHT LIKE

Chomping heaps of fluffy rice, meats and curries with your hands.

MIND YOUR LEAFWARE MANNERS! OR BANANA LEAVES AS PLATES

RECOMMENDED FOR

All things India, from flower garlands, to Indian snacks, *saris** and sparkling bangles.

VISIT LITTLE INDIA ARCADE: THE PLACE FOR ALL THINGS INDIAN

It's an utterly Singaporean ambition to be a hub for everything, be it food, transportation, entertainment or whatever else. That might explain why Little India Arcade touts itself as the hub for "all things Indian". Even better, it fulfils on its promise.

These Art Deco-style shophouses, built in 1913, sell all sorts of Indian fashion such as hand-embroidered *saris**, colourful shawls and sparkling bangles. But the true charm of the arcade lies in ferreting out activities that aren't as prevalent in the rest of Singapore.

Get a Henna tattoo, chomp on betel nuts (a mildly narcotic fruit that's supposedly good for digestion), adorn your car or hotel room with flower garlands made with jasmine, ixora and orchids; and don't forget to try *muruku** – a savoury Indian cracker – and Indian candies for that instant sugar rush.

CONSULT MANI THE PARAKEET WHO SEES ALL, PICKS ALL

The cards don't lie, according to the faithful Mani the Parakeet – the fortune-telling parrot. (Shhh... Mani and his handler, M. Muniyappan, are usually found along the corridor outside a restaurant in Little India.)

This rose-ringed parakeet divines the answer to your question by pecking on a card that's laid out before it. Even if you don't believe in fortune-telling, it's fun to watch the bird hop out of its cage and onto the table; eye the cards and pick one with its beak.

If you're wondering about Mani's accuracy, we'll have you know that the bird correctly predicted the winners of all of the 2010 World Cup quarter finals, as well as the Spain Germany semi-final!

Now that it's over, Mani has gone back to its daily grind of predicting lottery numbers, auspicious marriage dates, and your query for your future. Remember to keep it simple for the bird.

HEAD HERE TO

Watch the parakeet pick a card to answer your burning question.

CELEBRATE LIFE WITH HENNA TATTOOS

YOU MIGHT LIKE

Getting your hands covered with intricate Henna designs.

In the mood for a celebration? Stop by any beauty parlour in Little India Arcade and cover your hands with intricate Henna designs.

These temporary tattoos are traditionally worn by Indian women during festive occasions such as birthdays and weddings. And what better way to express your joy then with, and on, your hands?

The Henna tattoos are created via a process called Mehndi which involves staining the top layer of skin with a Henna paste product. Here's a tip: pick a Henna artist with steady hands. You wouldn't want to end up with whirls where there should be whorls.

It's almost impossible to remove the tattoos by scrubbing it off. But there's good news: they'll naturally fade away in about two to fours weeks.

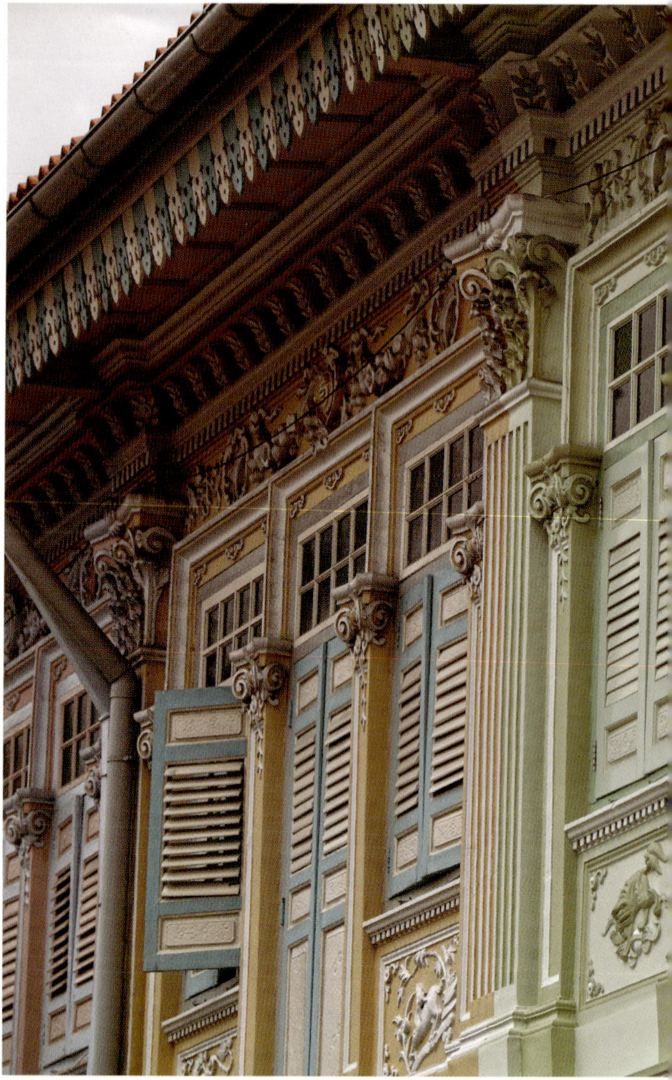

KATONG/ GEYLANG SERAI

Welcome to the (not-too-far-out) east of Singapore. Trade those uptown boots for lazy-hazy afternoons roaming the back lanes and *kopi tiams** of Katong, Joo Chiat and Geylang Serai. But first a little background...

Katong, Joo Chiat and Geylang Serai were the ethnic enclaves of various communities in the early 1900s, such as the Peranakans, Eurasians, and Malays. Like all good neighbours, these districts share friendly borders and stretch from Changi Road in Geylang Serai, to Joo Chiat Road, Ceylon Road and Koon Seng Road in Joo Chiat, up to East Coast Road in Katong.

We say head here to the east for its food, laid-back atmosphere and a slice of local life without the gloss. Joo Chiat and Katong are solidly middle-class neighbourhoods, so you'll find it most agreeable to wander around. The Peranakan shop house is ever-present in Katong and Joo Chiat (many of these are gazetted for conversation) so go ahead and snap away. At the heart of the area is Joo Chiat Road; once a dirt lane running through coconut plantations, today you'll find remnants of shady karaoke bars, a recent influx of creative companies, old-school eateries and religious landmarks rubbing shoulders.

Nearby Geylang Serai is Katong and Joo Chiat's less polished but no less colourful neighbour. Known as the "Malay Emporium" of Singapore, this is the area where the British ruling powers moved the original inhabitants of the island, the *Orang Lauts**. The Geylang Serai Market & Food Centre is at the heart of the action, where you'll find the largest variety of Malay dishes. Witness street and market life in its element, especially around the Hari Raya festivities where Changi Road decks out with chaotic outdoor bazaars.

THE SPOTS

___1 CHILLI PADI NONYA RESTAURANT
11 Joo Chiat Place #01-03
Singapore 486350
Tel: 6275 1002
www.chillipadi.com.sg

___2 CHIN MEI CHIN CONFECTIONERY
204 East Coast Road, Singapore 428903

___3 D'BUN THE HOMEMADE
BUN SPECIALIST
358 Joo Chiat Road, Singapore 427603
Tel: 6345 8220
www.dbun.com.sg

___4 ENG SENG RESTAURANT
247-249 Joo Chiat Place
Singapore 427935
Tel: 6440 5560

___5 FAMOUS 49 KATONG LAKSA
49 East Coast Road, Hock Tong Hin
Eating House, Singapore 428768
Tel: 6344 5101

___6 FEI FEI WANTON NOODLES
72 Joo Chiat Place, Singapore 427789
Tel: 6440 5013

___7 FOUR SEASONS DURIAN CAFÉ
43 Joo Chiat Place
Singapore 427922

___8 GEYLANG SERAI MARKET
& FOOD CENTRE
1 Geylang Serai, Singapore 402001

___9 HAJJAH MONA NASI PADANG
1 Geylang Serai #02-079
Geylang Serai Market & Food Complex
Singapore 402001

___10 JOO CHIAT COMPLEX
1 Joo Chiat Road, Singapore 420001

___11 KATONG ANTIQUE HOUSE
208 East Coast Road
Singapore 428907
Tel: 6345 8544

___12 KIM CHOO KUEH CHANG BABI
60 Joo Chiat Place, Singapore 427784
Tel: 6344 0830
www.kimchoo.com

___13 NAM SAN FOOD
MANUFACTURING
261 Joo Chiat Road, Singapore 427515
Tel: (65) 6345 5542
www.namsan.com.sg

___14 PUTERI MAS
475 Joo Chiat Road
Singapore 427682
Tel: 63448629
www.puterimas.com

___15 SINAR PAGI NASI PADANG
1 Geylang Serai #02-137
Geylang Serai Market & Food Complex
Singapore 402001

___16 SRI SENPAGA VINAYAGAR
TEMPLE
19 Ceylon Road
Singapore 429613
www.senpaga.org.sg

___17 TAN SWIE HIAN MUSEUM
460 Sims Avenue
Singapore 387601
Tel: 6744 0716
www.tanswiehian.com

EUNOS
PAYA LEBAR
sims avenue
changi road
geylang road
joo chiat terrace
joo chiat place
still road
joo chiat rd
onan road
carpmael rd
ceylon road
koon seng rd
pulasan rd
rambai rd
everitt rd
pennefather rd
tembeling road
duku road
haig ave
seraya lane
marshall road
ceylon road
carpmael road
onan road
fowlie rd
cheow keng rd
haig road
tanjong katong road
east coast road
sea ave
east coast road
marine parade road
mountbatten road
1
2
3
4
5
6
7
8
9
10
11
12
13
14
15
16
17

GORGE YOURSELF ON A KATONG FOOD TRAIL

This area is all about its food-glorious-food. Words along are not enough to do justice to Katong's authentic treats, so we beseech you to try everything (just once)...

Get going at the corner of Still Road and Joo Chiat Place: nothing beats sweating over black pepper crabs at Eng Seng Restaurant. Soldier down Joo Chiat Place to Fei Fei Wanton Noodles for a bowl of egg noodles. Yes, those triangular-shaped, banana-wrapped things are actually glutinous rice dumplings, or *nonya chang**, from Kim Choo Kueh Chang Babi.

We smell scrumptious Peranakan fare at Chilli Padi Nonya Restaurant; opposite, it's your initiation to the stinky (but some say delicious) durian fruit at Four Seasons Durian Café. Straight up is Joo Chiat Road: turn left and watch out for a rickety ol' store called Nam San Food Manufacturing selling fabulous *otah**.

More treats ahead – D'bun the Homemade Bun Specialist has pork and chicken *baos** that have captured the hearts of many a cab driver. Approaching East Coast Road, Puteri Mas is all about its Golden Durian Puffs. We'll be wrapping up our Katong food trail at one of these local haunts: now, will it be *kaya** toast at Chin Mei Chin Confectionery, or what-is-that-delicious-smell Katong *laksa** at Famous 49 Katong Laksa??

1. Four Seasons Durian Cafe 2. D'bun 3. Kim Choo Kueh Chang Babi 4. Fei Fei Wanton Noodles

115

GORGE YOURSELF ON A KATONG FOOD TRAIL

DID YOU

Get in your most adventurous food-tasting mood for *nonya chang**, *otah** and golden durian puffs?

ADMIRE THE ARCHITECTURE OF JOO CHIAT'S PERANAKAN HOUSES

Time to put on your flip flops and get lost in Joo Chiat – you could spend an afternoon here for one good reason – the Peranakan-styled houses.

Joo Chiat is chock-a-block with these historic gems. To snap a picture-perfect photo, make a beeline for the junction of Koon Seng Road and Joo Chiat Road. You'll find a row of brightly-coloured Art-deco Peranakan houses with fancy shutter windows and ceramic carvings. Wander around Joo Chiat Place, Joo Chiat Road, Tembeling Road and Crane Road to take in the eclectic style of these houses, with Chinese, Malay, Indian and European influences.

For an off-the- beaten-track experience, hunt down the dead end street starting at 150 East Coast Road for an interesting variation of the Peranakan house. This road used to be right by the beach before reclamation extended the land to today's East Coast Park. We love the staircases and raised level of the houses built to escape rising sea tides – you won't find these anywhere else.

DID YOU

Snap a photo of Art Deco Peranakan houses along picture-perfect Koon Seng Road?

DID YOU

Go giddy over *sarong kebayas**, Peranakan jewellery, beaded shoes and furnishings?

GO ON A WHIRLWIND TOUR OF PERANAKAN HERITAGE AT KATONG ANTIQUE HOUSE

This Peranakan mini-museum-store-home is truly an assault on the senses. Step into Katong Antique House and you'll go giddy with the Pernakan artefacts on display. There's ornate crockery, gorgeous *sarong kebayas**, sparkling jewellery, beaded shoes, faded portraits of *babas** and *bibiks** and large hanging lamps everywhere – where does one begin?

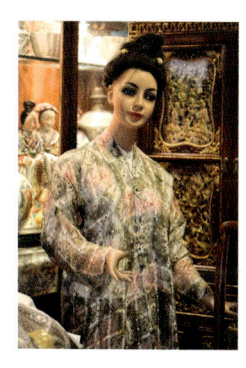

Don't fluster folks – while you're free to peer over the items, there's nothing quite like a personal tour. Find a group of five or more and Peter Wee, the curator and owner of Katong Antique House, will take you on a whirlwind 45-minute tour of this heritage house and gallery. At S$15 per person, you'll get to unravel the customs of a traditional Peranakan kitchen, ancestral hall and reception, admire an unrivalled collection that continues to grow after 25 years, and even be treated to Peranakan pastries and a spot of coffee or tea.

VISIT THE SRI SENPAGA VINAYAGAR TEMPLE

Tucked in quiet Ceylon Road, just off East Coast Road, here is one of the rare places to catch a glimpse of south Indian Chola architecture in Singapore. You'll recognise the temple by its terracotta and sandstone hues. This temple once suffered severe damage in a 1942 bombing during the Second World War. Fortunately, years of restoration efforts have reinstated the building to its former glory.

At the entrance, find a granite sculpture unique to ancient Chola temples. The majestic 4.5-metre teakwood doorway is based on Chola customs to accommodate kings of old riding in on elephants.

You'll have step in to view the temple's unique features from the main hall. Dress appropriately, wash your feet and you'll be allowed in. You won't find this even in India – admire the sculptures of 32 forms of Vinayagar on four main granite pillars; or peer at the 68-feet-high main tower, and the temple's gold-plated dome through two modern skylights.

DID YOU

Step inside to view the temple's sculptures of 32 forms of Vinayagar?

CELEBRATE A LIVING ARTIST AT THE TAN SWIE HIAN MUSEUM

Forget the post-humous fame of the tragic artist. Why not celebrate the living instead? There aren't many of this breed of museums in the world: the Tan Swie Hian Museum is one of those rare places that pays tribute to a living, working artist.

Painter-sculptor-calligrapher slash poet-critic-translator, Tan is the closest you're ever going to get to a Singaporean Renaissance man. The fourth floor of the Tomlinson Collection is dedicated to Tan's formidable's oeuvre. Did you know he was also conferred Knighthood by French Order of Arts and Letters in 1978 for his artistic achievements?

Expect an afternoon of sober, peaceful contemplation amidst refined art. Calligraphy etched on floors, philosophical chess pieces aloft, and contemporary oil and Chinese Ink paintings are some of the works on display by this 1987 Singaporean Cultural Medallion Winner.

DID YOU

Contemplate the works of painter-sculptor-calligrapher, Tan Swie Hian?

DID YOU

Admire the architecture styled like a Malay house?

SOAK IN THE ATMOSPHERE AT GEYLANG SERAI MARKET & FOOD CENTRE

If Geylang Serai is the original home of Singapore's Malay community, then this market is definitely its beating heart. Like *kampungs** of old, the Geylang Serai Market & Food Centre is styled rather like a traditional Malay House with its high sloping roofs, *batik** motifs and timber panels. Find your way here from street level, or via the overhead bridge from Joo Chiat Complex.

On the ground level is a broad veranda where you'll access all its market stalls where the crowded scenes of *makciks** haggling with the hawkers beats shopping at any typical supermarket. On the upper levels, find a mix of retail stores selling Malay clothing, accessories and the largest variety of Muslim-owned cooked food stores.

GO ETHNIC SHOPPING AT JOO CHIAT COMPLEX

Move over Orchard Road – a trip to Singapore isn't complete without exploring the fashion-styles of one of its largest racial groups. Joo Chiat Complex is your friendly Geylang Serai mall for all things Malay.

This is the locale for colourful Malay textiles, traditional costumes such as *baju kurungs** (for ladies) and *baju melayus** (for men), jewellery, ethnic crafts and souvenirs.

On the first level, find a dizzy assortment of textiles and curtain fabrics; poke around the upper levels for stores dedicated to ethnic-oriented items. If you happen to be in town around the Hari Raya Puasa holiday, come to Joo Chiat Complex to witness all the action. This sleepy building gets dressed up with festive decorations as it seems the whole Malay community heads here in full force to shop for spiffy new costumes for the holiday.

TRY NASI PADANG

DID YOU

Say "simply *sedap**" after a spot of beef *rendang**, *ayam lemak cili padi** or *bagedil**?

The many Muslim-owned stores at Geylang Serai Market & Food Centre makes this place a food haven for the Malay community. Your trip here wouldn't be complete without trying *nasi padang*, or rice served with a variety of side dishes. If that description sounds ordinary, the daunting queues at these two stores will tell you the *nasi padang** here is not.

At #02-079, Hajjah Mona Nasi Padang is run by Hajjah Mona herself. Lunch queues gather for her beef and chicken *rendang**, *lemak nangka**, *ayam lemak cili padi** and *ikan bakar**. Over at #02-137, Sinar Pagi Nasi Padang is a worthy rival with its delicious quail eggs in sambal chilli, *ayam bakar**, *lontong** and *bagedil**. Tuck in and find it simply *sedap**!

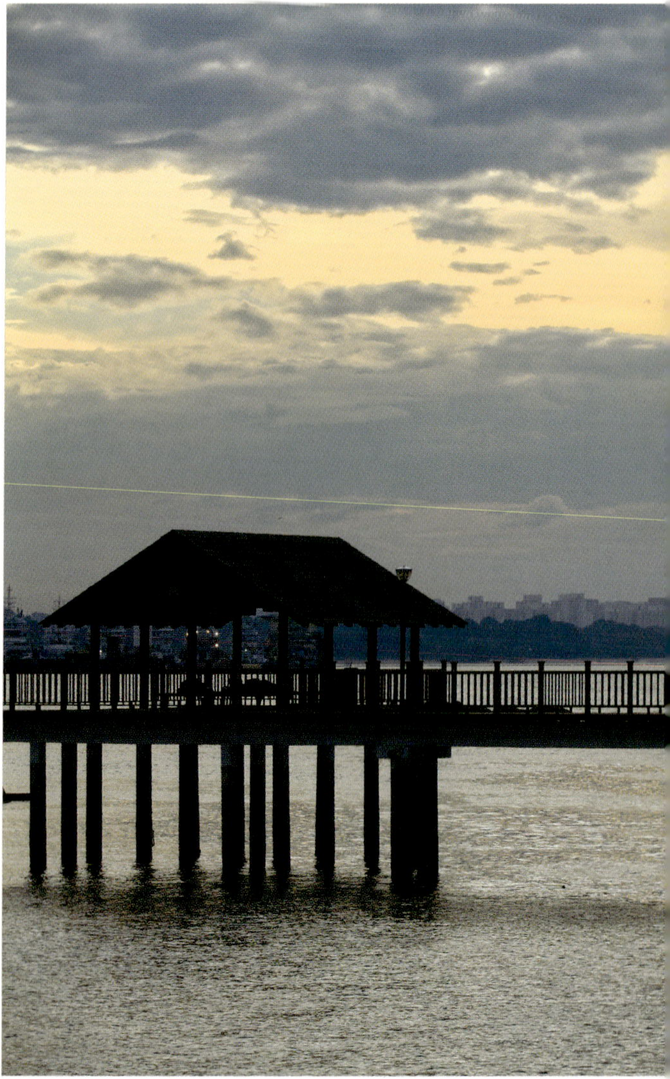

CHANGI/ PULAU UBIN

The larger-than-life Changi Airport may be your first welcome to our sunny island, but for the traveller willing to go the distance, Changi offers more than just your landing ground. Located on the far eastern point of Singapore, Changi has been described as "idllyic", "sleepy" and "breezy" – which really means lots of coastal sights, off the beaten track eateries and an overall laid-back atmosphere. Take a slow bus ride along route number 2 from Tanah Merah MRT (EW4) to reach Changi Village.

Changi houses a number of interesting historical locations. Locals will tell you about the abandoned Changi Hospital where few today dare to enter (rumours are rife about the wandering restless souls who died there during World War II). Changi Prison is in the vicinity; as well as Changi Cottage, a rustic house where Singapore's current Minister Mentor, Lee Kuan Yew, mulled over Singapore's future after the country's separation from Malaysia.

Changi Village is the area's most popular hang-out spot. Here's where you can eat at the famous Changi Village Market and Hawker Centre, catch a bumboat to Pulau Ubin from Changi Point Ferry Terminal, and embark on a 2.6-kilometre boardwalk along the Changi Point Coastal Walk. Pulau Ubin is a tiny island where you'll find some of the last villages in Singapore and is popular with visitors for fresh seafood, nature walks and cycling trips.

THE SPOTS

__1 CHANGI CHAPEL AND MUSEUM
1000 Upper Changi Road North
Singapore 507707
Tel: 6214 2451
www.changimuseum.com

__2 CHANGI POINT COASTAL WALK
From Changi Village to Changi Beach Club

__3 CHANGI POINT FERRY TERMINAL
51 Lorong Bekukong
Singapore 499172

__4 CHANGI VILLAGE MARKET AND HAWKER CENTRE
Block 2 Changi Village Road
Singapore 500002

__5 CHEK JAWA
For visitor information, visit chekjawa.nus.edu.sg and www.nparks.gov.sg.

__6 COOKERY MAGIC
Kampong House on Pulau Ubin
(Visit website for directions)
Tel: 6348 9667
www.cookerymagic.com

__7 INTERNATIONAL FOOD STALL
Block 2 Changi Village Road
#01-57,
Changi Village Market and Hawker Centre
Singapore 500002

__8 MIZZY'S CORNER
Block 2 Changi Village Road
#01-55,
Changi Village Market and Hawker Centre
Singapore 500002

__9 PULAU UBIN
For visitor information, visit www.nparks.gov.sg.

__10 SEASON LIVE SEAFOOD
59E Pulau Ubin
Singapore 508309
Tel: 6542 7627

__11 SRI SUJANA
Block 2 Changi Village Road
#01-54,
Changi Village Market and Hawker Centre
Singapore 500002

__12 UBIN FIRST STOP RESTAURANT
42 Pulau Ubin, Singapore 508293
Tel: 6543 2489
www.ubinfirststoprestaurant.com.sg

131

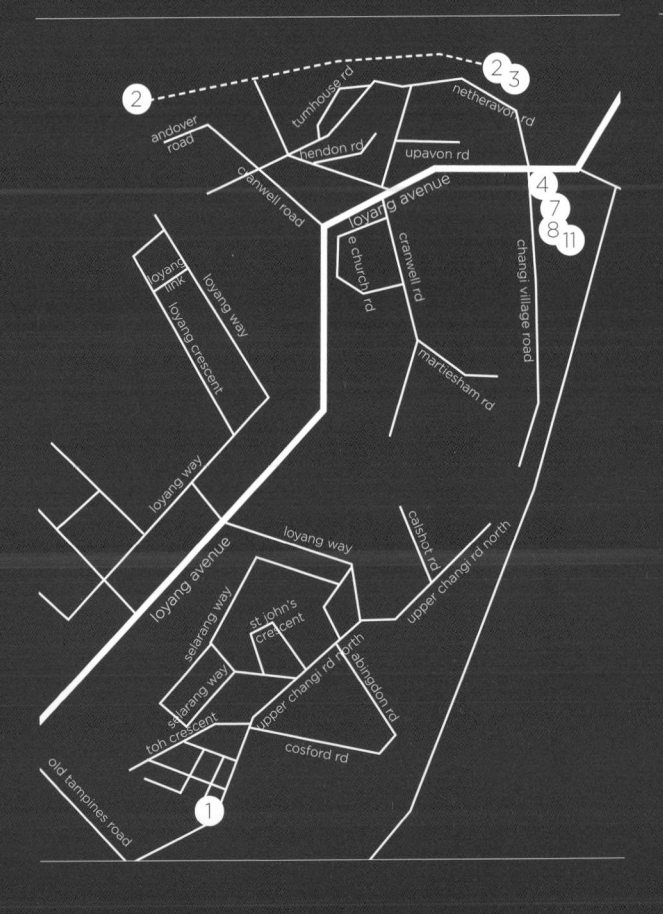

QUEUE UP FOR NASI LEMAK

DID YOU

Discover the fragrant aroma of *nasi lemak**'s coconut-infused rice?

Rice for dinner, lunch, and for breakfast. It's all rice in Singapore, and our "rice in cream", otherwise known as *nasi lemak**, tops our foodie list. At first glance, it's just a plate of rice with chopped up chicken wings, a crumpled fried egg, crispy anchovies by the side, and a massive dollop of red *sambal** on cucumber slices.

But at Changi Village Market and Hawker Centre, *nasi lemak** has become somewhat of a star attraction, with locals heading here from every corner of the island. You're going to have to beat the queues at International Food Stall, (#01-57), Sri Sujana (#01-54) and Mizzy's Corner (#01-55).

Nothing beats the sweet, rich aroma of the rice. The secret lies in steaming the rice in coconut cream and pandan leaves. This enriches each grain and infuses them with the coconut's fragrance. Now that's an ode to rice!

RECOUNT THE WAR YEARS AT CHANGI CHAPEL AND MUSEUM

Did you know that Changi was the captive site of many prisoners of war during Singapore's darkest years – the Japanese Occupation during the Second World War?

The quiet and unassuming Changi Chapel and Museum memorialises the stories of some 50,000 civilians and soldiers incacerated in Changi between 1942 to 1945. For visitors, it's a stirring and poignant glimpse into the daily lives of these unsung heroes.

Tales of prisoners cramped into tiny cells, those who painted murals of hope with meagre material, and men spurred on to live by quilts knitted by women prisoners are quietly told in the museum's hallowed halls. End your visit at the Changi Chapel in the middle of the museum to observe a moment of silence to remember those who triumphed over adversity.

DID YOU

Unravel the poignant stories of Singapore's prisoners of war during the Japanese Occupation?

NATURE WALK AT CHEK JAWA

What goes on under the boardwalk, down by the shore at Chek Jawa? Listen to the nature pundits: Chek Jawa's wetlands are one of Singapore's last outposts for observing flora, fauna and marine life. It packs an incredible number of ecosystems, from mangroves, to forests, rocky shores, seagrass lagoons, and coral rubble.

Located at the south-eastern coast of Pulau Ubin, you'll have to either bike, hire a van or walk 40-minutes to reach Chek Jawa. It's a bit of a rough-and-tumble experience (read: no nearby toilets or shelter, so stock up on water and umbrellas). Experts recommend coming here at low-tide (when it's easiest to observe the wildlife) but you'll need to check out the best times at www.nparks.gov.sg.

It certainly won't be easy to find Nemo in this thriving marshlands. But walk along the one-kilometre boardwalk to say hello to Chek Jawa's residents, from horse shoe crabs, sand dollars, nudibranches, anemones and endangered sea grasses. Reach the high-viewing tower to take in the spectacular view of the wetlands.

DID YOU

Come during low-tide when it's easiest to observe the unique wildlife?

Spot a horse shoe crab, sand dollar, nudibranch, or anemone?

CYCLE AROUND PULAU UBIN

Singapore is 137-square-kilometres of city sights, so where does one go to experience a little bit of the countryside? There's good news: get on the bumboat at Changi Point Ferry Terminal, at Singapore's south-eastern coast, to get to this relatively idllyic island. And the best way to get around Pulau Ubin? Cycling. There are bicycle shops galore around the jetty to get you going.

But don't expect an easy ride. The island is known for its dirt tracks and some steep slopes so remember to check the bicycle brakes before you leave the jetty. Ask for a map, spray on some mosquito repellent, and you're set. Take in the last vestiges of village life in Singapore and abandoned granite quarries (once the main trade on the island) admist lush forest surroundings.

DID YOU

Explore this idyllic island and the last vestiges of village life in Singapore?

GET SOME LOVIN' ON THE CHANGI POINT COASTAL WALK

The Drifters have a strange idea of fine lovin' in their song, *Under the Boardwalk*:

"Oh, when the sun beats down and burns the tar up on the roof
And your shoes get so hot you wish your tired feet were fire-proof
Under the boardwalk, down by the sea, yeah
On a blanket with my baby is where I'll be."

We've got our own version of The Drifters' notion of romance: the 2.6km Changi Point Coastal Walk stretches from Changi Village to Changi Beach Club.

Instead of hiding under the boardwalk like a troll, you and your partner should stroll on it. The Changi Point Coastal Walk will take you past views of sailboats, through shady coniferous trees, and a short jaunt over the sea before it opens into a deck that faces the setting sun.

Now that's romance for you. PS: The sunsets are gorgeous. So time it right!

DID YOU

Time it right to catch the sunsets along the Changi Point Coastal Walk?

GORGE ON FRESH SEAFOOD AT PULAU UBIN

Why would anyone traverse Singapore, hitch a bumboat ride across the sea to devour seafood on a tiny island? That's what some Singaporeans do on weekends (the rest cycle around the island before tucking into seafood).

Just what draws them to Pulau Ubin's restaurants such as Ubin First Stop Restaurant and Season Live Seafood?

It's all about fresh seafood cooked simply, like prawns battered with butter and fried, or a perfectly steamed seabass with preserved soybeans. Round off dinner with an order of chilli crabs set amidst rustic surroudings – wooden balconies, plastic chairs and tables, uneven floor boards and balmy sea breezes for a winning dinner.

DID YOU

Indulge in a round of butter battered prawns, steam seabass and chilli crabs?

WHIP UP A FEAST… IN PULAU UBIN'S JUNGLE

DID YOU

Traipse into the jungle for freshly harvested herbs?

Cooking classes are a dime a dozen on mainland Singapore. But preparing a dish of *nasi kerabu** with herbs freshly harvested from the jungle? Now that's an experience that's hard to come by, especially in urban Singapore.

That's what you'll get at Ruqxana's cooking classes. The chef-owner of Cookery Magic takes her students out of the studio and into Pulau Ubin's jungle where she'll show you how jungle herbs such as *daun teh** and *daun belingau** are used in traditional Malay cooking.

Rest assured that while you'll be traipsing through the jungle for herbs, you won't have to cook outdoors. Ruqxana conducts all of her classes indoors, albeit in a 100-year old *kampong** house. But you'll need to book ahead as spaces are limited – Ruqxana only holds classes on Pulau Ubin on the last Saturday of each month. Visit www.cookerymagic.com for details.

SENTOSA

Singapore's closest thing to a nearby getaway, Sentosa used to be a sleepy island the south of Singapore, frequented by school children, families and beach buffs. The most magical sighting was a musical fountain that danced to the changing beats; while beach-starved Singaporeans embraced the sandy beaches to volley, tan, and frolic in the ocean.

Sentosa still retains an island resort atmosphere, but it has changed gears into a powerhouse attraction with the opening of Resorts World Sentosa in early 2010. Run by the illustrious Genting Group, Resorts World Sentosa packs a high-roller casino, Southeast Asia's first Universal Studios Singapore® theme park, and the Marina Life Park, billed as the largest oceanarium in the world. Those seeking a thrill pill can hurtle down a flying fox ride (MegaZip Adventure Park), cart down a hill (Sentosa Luge & Skyride) or fly in the air on a trapeze (The Flying Trapeze).

To the south-east, the Serapong and the Tanjong golf courses are billed as championship gold courses that attract the very best in the game. The mainstays of Siloso Beach, Palawan Beach and Tanjong Beach still offer fun in the sun, though it's dotted with more activities and chi-chi bars than before (make a beeline for Café Del Mar and Tanjong Beach Club). When the excitement of the day is over, amble across the bridge on Palawan Beach to watch the sun set at the southern-most point of Continental Asia.

143

THE SPOTS

1 AZZURA BEACH CLUB
46 Siloso Beach Walk
Sentosa
Singapore 099005
Tel: 6270 8003
www.azzura.sg

2 FISH REFLEXOLOGY, UNDERWATER WORLD
80 Siloso Road
Sentosa
Singapore 098969
Tel: 6279 9229
www.underwaterworld.com.sg/fishreflex.htm

3 IMAGES OF SINGAPORE
40 Imbiah Road
Singapore 099700
Tel: 1800 736 8672

4 JEWEL CABLE CAR RIDE
109 Mount Faber Road
The Jewel Box
Singapore 099203
Tel: 6377 9688
www.mountfaber.com.sg

5 RESORTS WORLD SENTOSA
39 Artillery Avenue
Sentosa
Singapore 099958
Tel: 6577 8888 (General);
Tel: 6577 8899 (Reservations and Ticketing)
www.rwsentosa.com

6 SENTOSA LUGE & SKYRIDE
45 Siloso Beach Walk
Imbiah Lookout (Beside Beach Station), Sentosa
Singapore 099003
www.hg.sg/sentosa/luge

7 WAVE HOUSE SENTOSA
36 Siloso Beach Walk
Sentosa, Singapore 099007
Tel: 6377 3113
www.wavehousesentosa.com

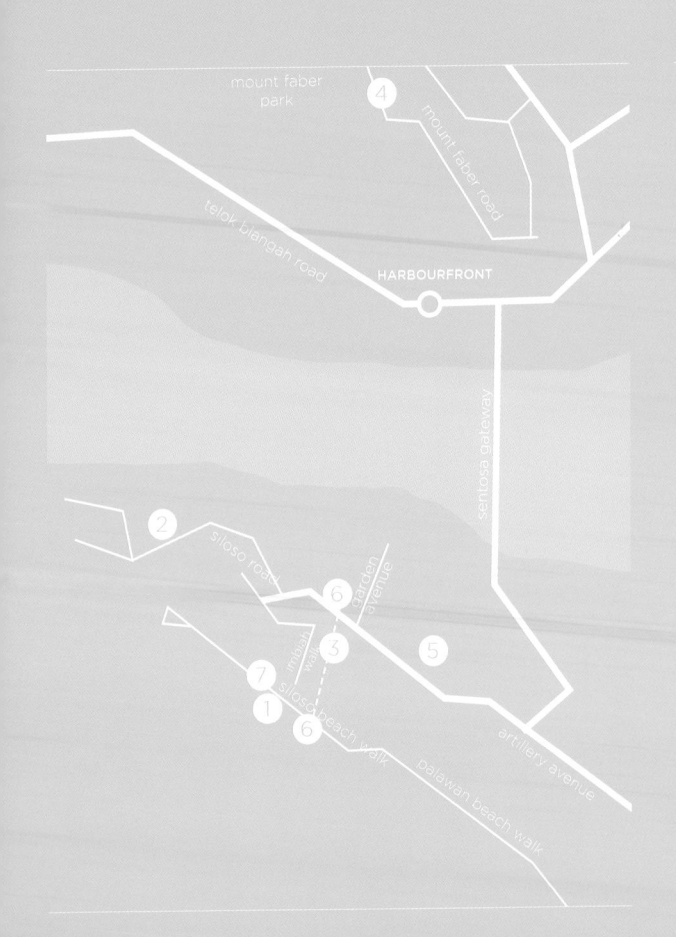

CATCH A CABLE CAR RIDE

WORTH A VISIT

To catch panoramic sky views of Harbourfront and Sentosa island.

One can cross the sea to nearby Sentosa island by ferry or traverse a bridge by car or bus, but by far the most interesting way to get there is by air. No, Sentosa isn't far enough to warrant a jet plane, but you'll still feel on top of the world in a cable car taking you from the top of Mount Faber across Harbourfront to the arrival hall at Sentosa.

The trusty old cable car has gotten an upgrade: now known as the Jewel Cable Car Ride from The Jewel Box, the cables now give passengers a more comfortable ride. Baby prams and wheelchairs can be rolled in easily, while the panoramic windows give you more views for your buck.

P.S. The cable car rides aren't just for merrymakers to Sentosa. The operators offer Sky Dining: watch the sun set 100 feet in the air as you tuck into a three-course meal.

GET FISH FOOT THERAPY AT UNDERWATER WORLD

YOU MIGHT LIKE

Watching the happy fish nibble away the dead skin on your feet.

In Singapore, de-stressing treatments of all sorts abound from Swedish to Thai massages and everything in-between. But the most memorable, unusual and pain-free treatments are those given by fish – specifically Turkish spa fish (aka *Garra rufa*) at Sentosa's Fish Reflexology, Underwater World.

These tiny fish imported from the Middle East have a taste for calluses on the feet. So what happens is that they'll nibble away at dead skin like benign piranhas. The entire process is quite simple: all you have to do is just dunk your feet into the fish tanks, feed the fish with your feet, and when time's up, get ready for a rub down by the foot reflexologists.

P.S. The fishes' nibbling tickles. Try not to laugh too loudly.

WORTH A VISIT

To ride a roller coaster at Universal Studios Singapore®, catch circus performances at Voyage de la Vie and visit the world's largest oceanarium.

GO ON A BIG DAY OUT AT RESORTS WORLD SENTOSA

Searching for your inner Peter Pan? Here's a solution: spend time at the family-friendly attractions at Resorts World Sentosa.

There are the Universal Studios Singapore® rides which include trips to Shrek's home in Far Far Away, and Monster Rock – a monster spooktacular filled with fireworks. Or take in the resort's version of Cirque du Soliel at the Voyage de la Vie where circus performers prance and contort on and off the stage. Wildlife folks should make a beeline for Marine Life Park, an oceanarium billed as the world's largest where you can interact with reef fishes, and the Maritime Xperiential Museum that details the Maritime Silk Route.

Folks with itchy fingers can hit up the casino. Do head to the smorgasbord of restaurants that range from casual (e.g. Chilli's Grill & Bar and Ruyi's) to fine-dining (e.g. Chinois by Susur Lee and kunio tokuoka) to satiate growling stomachs.

PUMP, JUMP, SPIKE AND SURF AT SENTOSA'S BEACHES

Sentosa island is Singapore's answer to Phuket or Koh Samui. Like both islands, Sentosa has a wide variety of beach sport activities to sweat it out under the sun. The place for these activities is Siloso Beach.

There are volleyball courts dredged into the sand for tanned boys and girls in fives and threes to spike volleyballs. Check with the pubs for court usage. If getting sand on your face isn't your thing, then head to AZZURA Beach Club, a hydrosports complex where you can rent canoes, banana boats and kayaks for your peddling pleasure.

Wave junkies can ride 10-foot tall waves at the Wave House Sentosa which simulates cowabunga surf-high waves and tubes. If the surf's too massive, we suggest a jaunt with our local skim boarding tribe at Palawan Beach.

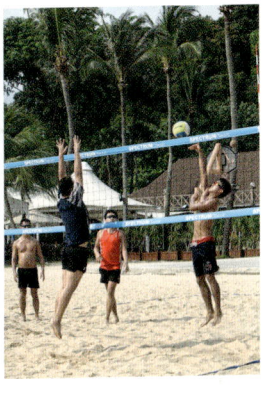

DID YOU

Head out to sea in a canoe, banana boat or kayak or sweat it out over a game of beach volleyball?

PUMP, JUMP, SPIKE AND SURF AT SENTOSA'S BEACHES

RELEASE YOUR INNER KID ON THE SENTOSA LUGE

WORTH A VISIT

To zip downhill over 600 metres of tropical terrain in a luge.

This ride isn't just for the kids – you're likely to find both young and old queuing for a ride on the Sentosa Luge & Skyride. The Sentosa Luge combines a nifty go-cart, over 600 metres of tropical terrain, and a hill, using good old gravity to send you hurtling downhill in troops.

Simply put: it's a wholesome and stress-free way to release your inner kid. All you have to do is control the luge (it's got a fuss-free steering and braking system) as you zip down the bends on the Jungle Trail or Dragon Trail. Simulate the feeling of Singapore's Formula One Night Race with a night luge ride. It's minutes of pure unadulterated fun that'll leave you wanting take two – that's why there's a four-seater sky ride to take you back up the hill right where you started.

VISIT IMAGES OF SINGAPORE

RECOMMENDED FOR

A journey through Singapore's history with life-sized figures and multimedia displays.

History maketh a country. But it doesn't mean we have to learn about it from pieces of parchment enshrined behind glass blocks. At the Images of Singapore (Imbiah Lookout), Singapore's past comes to life with multimedia displays, theatre presentations and life-sized figurines.

You'll get a chronological rendering of Singapore's history from its earliest days to the present, with exhibitions that cover Zhang He's discovery of old Singapore; Sir Stamford Raffles' founding of the city-state; the Japanese Occupation; and the post-colonial era under Lee Kuan Yew, Singapore's first Prime Minister. Each exhibit is explained by interactive videos.

The icing on the cake is the multimedia show: "Four Winds of Singapore" – a tribute to the Chinese, Indian, Malay and Eurasians – where their story is narrated by a girl's holographic image and special effects which bring her tale to three-dimensional life.

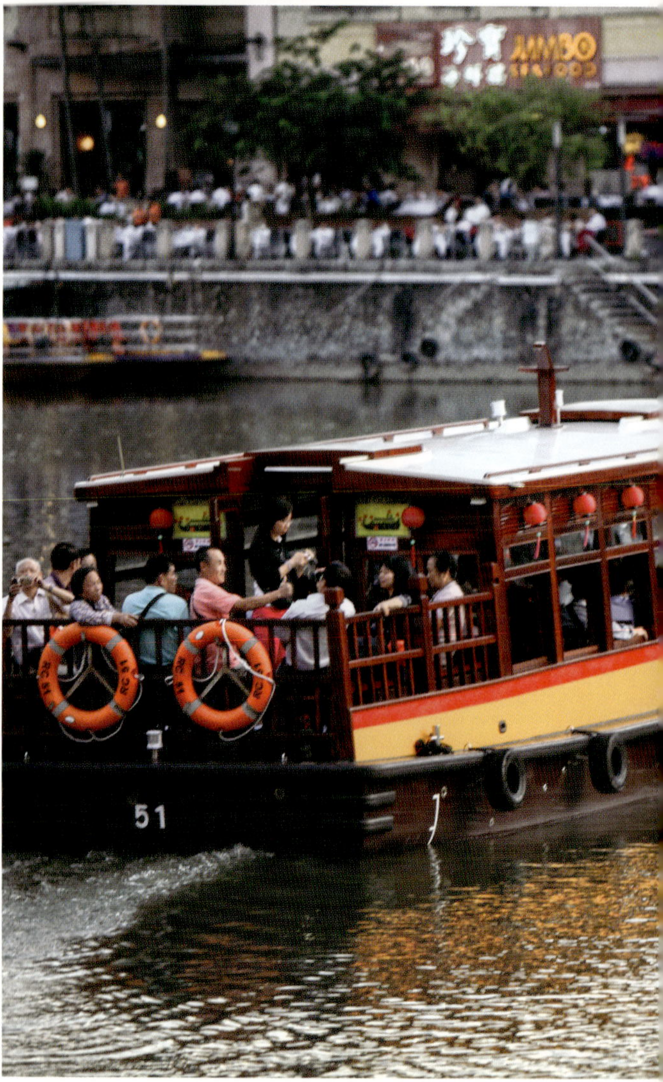
51

THE QUAYS

Singapore's most popular strip of bars and restaurants spans over three quays – Boat Quay, Clarke Quay and Robertson Quay. They are connected via pathways that meander along the Singapore River. But it's rare to see folks wander from quay to quay as each area caters to different niches with their peculiar offerings.

The Shenton Way gang head to Boat Quay's pubs after a day of financial haggling and trading – reminiscent of Boat Quay's past as a centre for shipping businesses in the 1860s. And the grand old lady caters to all with her bawdy bars: expats cluster over pints of Old Speckled Hen in waterfront bars; whilst locals bawl ballads and lord over jugs of Tiger beer in KTV Pubs along Circular Road.

Clarke Quay, a 10-minute walk through underpasses and over busy bridges, attracts camera-wielding tourists and well-heeled professionals. The aged grain and who-knows-what's-in-them warehouses now spot pastel coats of paint and swanky restaurants that serve western bloc cuisines. Unlike Boat Quay, the area's pubs and discos are less rowdy but quirkier.

Further on lies Robertson Quay. This once-boisterous stretch of clubs (and before that a muddy swamp land) is gentrified by dining spots where tinkling glass and cutlery prevail. It's stuffed by predominantly Japanese restaurants that host an incredible selection of Sake, Shochu and Awamori and European-style bistros. For pulse-pounding action, clubbers need only saunter past this quiet part of the river to grand dame of clubs: Zouk.

THE SPOTS

___ 1 BAR BAR BLACK SHEEP
86 Robertson Quay, Singapore 238245
Tel: 6836 9255
www.bbbs.com.sg

___ 2 BREWERKZ RIVERSIDE POINT
30 Merchant Road #01-05/06,
Riverside Point, Singapore 058282
Tel: 6438 7438
www.brewerkz.com

___ 3 BRUSSELS SPROUTS
80 Mohamed Sultan Road
#01-12, The Pier at Robertson Quay
Singapore 239013
Tel: 6887 4344
www.brusselssprouts.com.sg

___ 4 LAURENT'S CAFÉ AND BAR
80 Mohamed Sultan Road
#01-11, The Pier at Robertson Quay
Singapore 239013
Tel: 6235 9007
www.thechocolatefactoryonline.com

___ 5 LUNAR ASIAN FUSION BAR
Block 3C, The Cannery
River Valley Road #01-03
Clarke Quay
Singapore 179022
Tel: 6305 6767
www.lunar.sg

___ 6 MENYA SHINCHAN JAPANESE NOODLE RESTAURANT
30 Robertson Quay #01-05
Riverside View, Singapore 238251
Tel: 6732 0114

___ 7 PITSTOP CAFÉ
14B Circular Road, Singapore 049370
Tel: 6535 5383
www.pitstopcafe.com.sg

___ 8 SETTLERS CAFÉ
39 North Canal Road, Singapore 059295
Tel: 6535 0435
www.settlerscafe.com

___ 9 SINGAPORE TYLER PRINT INSTITUTE
41 Robertson Quay Singapore 238236
Tel: 6336 3663
www.stpi.com.sg

___ 10 THE CLINIC
Block 3C, The Cannery
River Valley Road #01-03, Clarke Quay
Singapore 179022
Tel: 6887 3733
www.theclinic.sg

___ 11 THE CHUPITOS BAR
Block 3C, The Cannery
River Valley Road #01-02 Clarke Quay
Singapore 179022
www.thechupitosbar.com

___ 12 THE MIND CAFÉ
68 Boat Quay, Singapore 049856
Tel: 6334 4427
www.themindcafe.com.sg

___ 13 ZOUK CLUB
17 Jiak Kim Street, Singapore 169420
Tel: 6738 2988
www.zoukclub.com

159

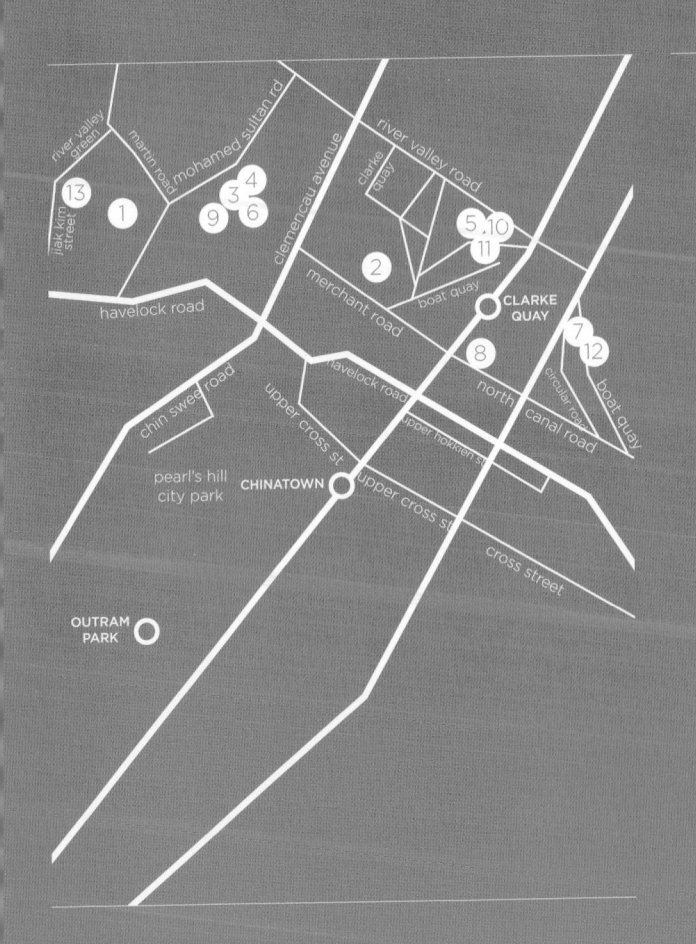

PARTY AT ZOUK

On your Singapore clubbing circuit, Zouk is probably your best initiation to the local clubbing culture. A Singaporean institution, the club has received many illustrious international reviews and played host to gigs by Bjork, DJ Paul Olkenfold and The Chemical Brothers.

Head here where the crowds are always finely dressed, and where the DJs keep it tight with progressive dance music. The club is divided into four distinct spaces: Zouk, the largest dance floor area spinning a mix of dance and house music; slinky Phuture where party animals gyrate to a wicked set of R&B and hip hop; loungy Velvet Underground for a more sophisticated crowd; and Wine Bar with its outdoor seating for a spot of drinks before a night of revelry. Don't miss Mambo Jambo on Wednesday nights where the retro lovers will hog the podiums and perform strange and amazingly synchronised dance moves to popular 70s and 80s hits (Think *Love in the First Degree* by Bananarama and *YMCA* by the Village People).

DID YOU

Grab drinks at Winebar before partying at either Zouk, Phuture or Velvet Underground?

GO BAR-HOPPING AT CLARKE QUAY

YOU MIGHT LIKE

Clarke Quay's concentration of bars, perfect for happy hour.

Some decry Clarke Quay as Singapore's mecca of tourist congeniality and drunkenness, but it also boasts the largest concentration of bars in this city-state for fun, booze and happy hours.

We'd recommend The Clinic for its morbid take on a good night out with red-coloured alcohol sipped from IV drips and wheelchairs for seats. For in-between dinner and club-hopping drinks, down shots at The Chupitos Bar, dedicated to creative shooters such as the Milo Dinosaur and Kiss of Death. Beer folks should try the craft beers at Brewerkz.

For clubbing fun, Lunar Asian Fusion Bar caters to Cantopop lovers with their live band and sultry dancers, but we can't shake off feeling like we're in a Hong Kong triad film.

1, 2. The Clinic
3. Lunar Asian Fusion Bar

HANG OUT AT BOARD GAME CAFES

REMEMBER TO

Seek recommendations on board games from the staff.

This might make the list on your night owl shifts. Board game cafes have caught on in Singapore, and are great for group affairs. For one, these cafes are affordable, provide hours of entertainment, and they stay open till the wee hours. The concept is simple: order a drink, dessert or meal, pay a package fee, choose a board game and you're set.

Popular with a younger crowd, the challenge comes in choosing what games to play. Seek recommendations from the staff, who might be able to teach you how to play. Literary types are likely to gravitate towards games like Taboo, or Upwords; while more cerebral individuals might fancy a strategy or memory game. Then there are games which bring out everyone's competitive side (like Ugly Dolls, where the winner is the one who snatches the most matching cards), all in the name of fun, of course. Check out the various popular card game cafes along the Singapore River – including The Mind Café and Pitstop Café at Boat Quay, and Settlers Café at Clarke Quay.

1,2,3,4. Mind Cafe

HANG OUT AT BOARD GAME CAFES

163

YOU MIGHT LIKE

Al fresco dining nights at Robertson Quay by the river

DINE AT ROBERTSON QUAY'S RESTAURANTS

Dining at Robertson Quay is all about the area's moderated charms – it's central without being too crowded, has a good selection of restaurants without being too flashy, and a relaxed atmosphere without losing its class. The restaurants enjoy a proximity to the river bank, so head here for *al fresco* nights amidst a genial atmosphere...

Menya Shinchan Japanese Noodle Restaurant has been faithfully serving the Japanese expatriate community its warm, authentic bowls of delicious handmade *ramen* noodles and some of the widest range of *ramen* broths in town. For the most decadent fluffy soufflés, chocolate tarts and smooth lattes, Laurent's Café and Chocolate Bar is a casual yet chic café that exudes a passion for pastries. The aptly named restaurant Brussels Sprouts is where one can get a decent Belgian beer (around 120 types available) and a fresh round of mussels cooked in an astounding variety of flavours. Watering hole Bar Bar Black Sheep has kept customers happy with its unique concept – offering Thai, Western and Indian food under one roof, a good burger and affordable beer.

1,2. Brussels Sprouts
3. Laurent Café & Chocolate Bar
4. Bar Bar Black Sheep

MARVEL CONTEMPORARY PRINTS AT THE SINGAPORE TYLER PRINT INSTITUTE

For art lovers interested in printed works, the Singapore Tyler Print Institute (STPI) is an art institution with a particular edge. This unassuming gallery by the banks of Robertson Quay is a hotbed of artistic activity in printmaking and papermaking. Established in 2002 under the guidance of American master printer Kenneth E. Tyler, the STPI has developed unique facilities and equipment attracting artists around the world to push the possibilities of paper.

For visitors, the ongoing and eclectic range of exhibitions held by artists-in-residences is a draw. For collectors, it's a good place to survey and buy new print works created at the STPI, from artists such as photographer Russell Wong, contemporary artist Ashley Bickerton, and Chinese artist, Wilson Shieh. For paper enthusiasts, the STPI conducts a range of workshops throughout the year in techniques such as mixed media print making, etching, screen printing and lithography.

CHECK OUT

The ongoing and eclectic range of paper and printmaking exhibitions.

BUMBOAT DOWN THE SINGAPORE RIVER

REMEMBER TO

Bring along your best camera to capture sights along the river.

Bumboats are a throwback to Singapore's colonial past. History tells us Sir Thomas Stamford Raffles arrived in 1819 at the Singapore River, foreseeing the island's potential as a port for entrepot trade. These rickety bumboats were ubiquitous along the river bed in the 1800s, mostly used to ferry goods from ships in the outer seas to warehouses along the river banks.

Fast forward to the 21st century and Singapore's answer to London's Thames, New York's Hudson and Melbourne's Yarra is no longer the lifeblood of the country's trade activity. The government has massively cleaned up the river where congestion and pollution were once rife. The bumboats will now take you through some of the most stunning areas in the central business district, the happening bar and club area of Clarke Quay and the dramatic Marina Bay area. Just book a ride at www.rivercruise.com.sg, or call (+65) 6336 6111 or (+65) 6336 6119.

COLONIAL DISTRICT

Walking around Singapore's colonial district today, you'll find historical buildings jostling next to commercial malls, a slew of museums, and the central business district. The colonial district is generally walkable, so exit from the City Hall, Raffles Place or Dhoby Ghaut train stations. Malls dot the area so you can easily head indoors for a drink and cool air.

With its proximity to the Singapore River, the colonial district became a site of many early centres of governance and commerce under British colonial rule. Sir Stamford Raffles, who founded the city of Singapore, lived in a bungalow, a fairly large residence which served as a home to subsequent Governors atop Fort Canning Hill; today, Fort Canning is a lush green park. Admire the Victorian and Neo-Palladian style of architecture at The Supreme Court, City Hall and the Old Parliament House; and also at the famous Raffles Hotel, which once hosted stars the likes of Charlie Chaplin, Michael Jackson, Queen Elizabeth II, and Somerset Maugham.

Bright and bustling, there's much to see and do in the colonial district. Many of Singapore's best museums are within walking distance from each other; while bars and dining outlets are aplenty. Don't forget to appreciate Singapore's increasingly dramatic city skyline via these choice routes: rooftop bars, down the river in a bumboat or on a trishaw.

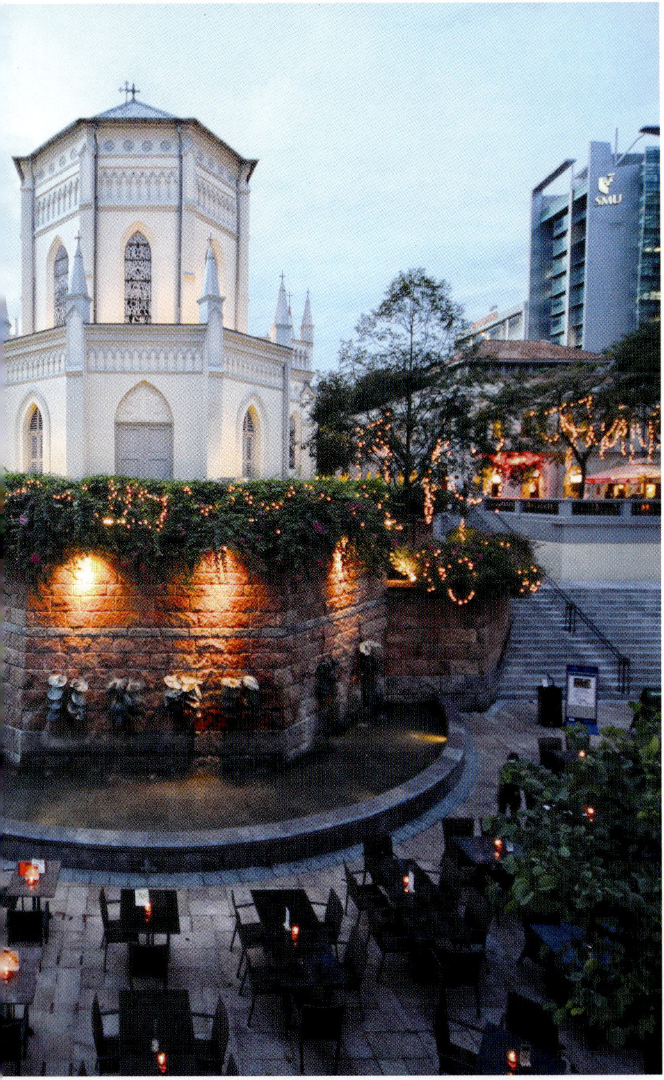
SMU

THE SPOTS

___ 1 ASIAN CIVILISATIONS MUSEUM
1 Empress Place, Singapore 179555
Tel: 6332 2982
www.acm.org.sg

___ 2 BATTLE BOX
2 Cox Terrace, Singapore 179622
Tel: 6333 0510

___ 3 CIVIL DEFENCE HERITAGE GALLERY
62 Hill Street
Singapore 179367
Tel: 6332 2996
www.scdf.gov.sg

___ 4 FORT CANNING PARK
Cox Terrace Singapore 179618
Tel: 6332 1200
www.nparks.gov.sg

___ 5 ESPLANADE – THEATRES ON THE BAY
1 Esplanade Drive, Singapore 038981
Tel: 6828 8377
www.esplanade.com

___ 6 ESMIRADA @ CHIJMES
30 Victoria Street #01-17
Chijmes, Singapore 187996
Tel: 6336 3684
www.esmirada.com

___ 7 INSOMNIA BAR & RESTAURANT
30 Victoria Street #01-21/22/23
Chijmes, Singapore 187996
Tel: 6334 4693

8 LE BAROQUE
30 Victoria Street
#B1-07, Fountain Court Chijmes
Singapore 187996
Tel: 6339 6696
www.lebaroque.com.sg

9 LONG BAR, RAFFLES HOTEL
1 Beach Road, Singapore 189673
Tel: 6412 1816
www.raffles.com

10 LOOF
331 North Bridge Road #03-07
Odeon Towers Extension Rooftop
Singapore 188720
Tel: 6338 8035
www.loof.com.sg

11 MAKANSUTRA GLUTTONS BAY
8 Raffles Avenue #01-15
Singapore 039802
www.makansutra.com/eateries_mgb.html

12 NATIONAL MUSEUM OF SINGAPORE
93 Stamford Road
Singapore 178897
Tel: 6332 3659
www.nationalmuseum.sg

13 NEW ASIA BAR
2 Stamford Road
Level 71, Swissôtel The Stamford
Singapore 178882
Tel: 6837 3322

14 ORGO
1 Esplanade Drive
#04-01, Roof Terrace
Esplanade – Theatres on the Bay
Singapore 038981
Tel: 6336 9366
www.orgo.sg

15 PERANAKAN MUSEUM
39 Armenian Street, Singapore 179941
Tel: 6332 7591; 6332 2982; 6332 3275
www.peranakanmuseum.sg

16 SINGAPORE ART MUSEUM
71 Bras Brasah Road
Singapore 189555
Tel: 6332 3222
www.singaporeartmuseum.sg

17 SINGAPORE PHILATELIC MUSEUM
23-B Coleman Street
Singapore 179807
Tel: 6337 3888
www.spm.org.sg

18 TABLE 108
30 Victoria Street
#B1-08, Fountain Court Chijmes
Singapore 187996
Tel: 6338 6108

19 THE SUBSTATION
45 Armenian Street
Singapore 179936
Tel: 6337 7535
www.substation.org

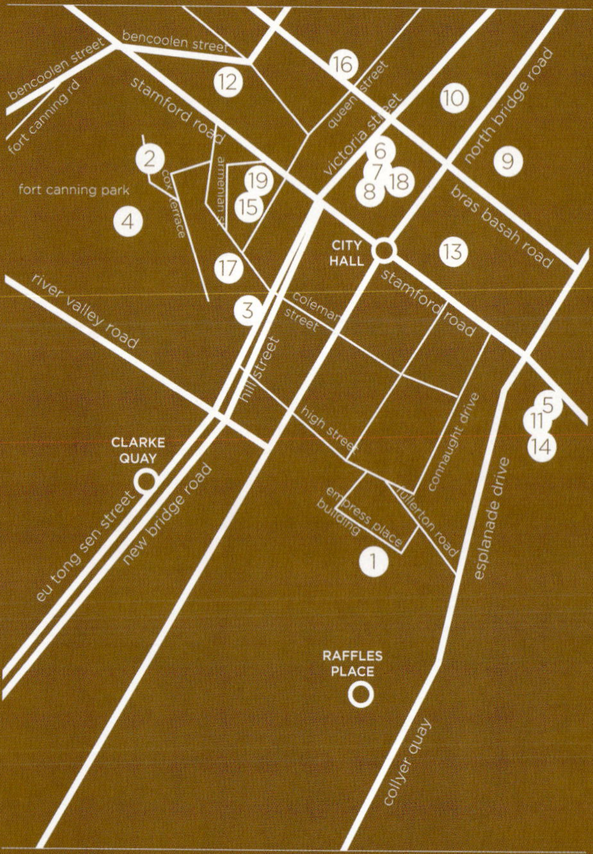
bencoolen street
bencoolen street
fort canning rd
stamford road
fort canning park
cox terrace
armenian st
queen street
victoria street
north bridge road
bras basah road
CITY HALL
stamford road
river valley road
coleman street
hill street
high street
connaught drive
esplanade drive
CLARKE QUAY
eu tong sen street
new bridge road
empress place building
fullerton road
RAFFLES PLACE
collyer quay
1
2
3
4
5
6
7
8
9
10
11
12
13
14
15
16
17
18
19

TAKE YOUR KIDS TO A FIRE STATION AT THE CIVIL DEFENCE HERITAGE GALLERY

DID YOU

Discover old fire-fighting equipment such as the Merryweather Fire King?

It's a lovely place to take your kids to learn about fire fighting – the Central Fire Station, Singapore's oldest fire station, is a beautiful colonial-styled red and white building along Hill Street.

Built in 1908, this national monument also houses the Civil Defence Heritage Gallery, where you'll be privy to vintage firefighting equipment (watch out for the Merryweather Fire King, Singapore's first fully motorised fire-engine); and probably learn a thing or two about handling real-life fire emergencies through the Gallery's public education displays. History is remembered here too, including the Bukit Ho Swee fire which destroyed 2,200 attap houses in 1961.

You might like the special Tower Tour, which will give you a chance to go up the Central Fire Station's 30-metre-tall watch tower where firemen once kept vigil on the area in the 1990s.

To book a tour at the Civil Defence Heritage Gallery or the Tower Tour, call (+65) 6332 2996 two weeks in advance or online at www.scdf.gov.sg.

GET A 101 ON SINGAPORE'S HISTORY AT THE NATIONAL MUSEUM OF SINGAPORE

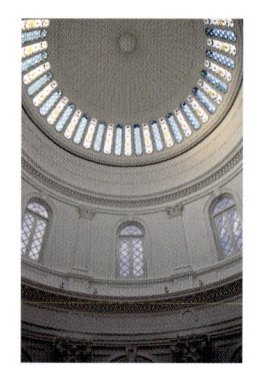

What is the Singapore story? For those curious about the history of this (very) young nation, Singapore's oldest museum, the National Museum of Singapore (NSM), may offer an insight.

The permanent exhibitions at the NSM dig deep into the past, from the 14th century, through to the time of 19th century colonial rule, till the nation-building years in the 1960s. From sleepy fishing village, to busy port, to powerhouse of Southeast Asia, Singapore has changed dramatically since its founding. Hear the stories of national struggle and the voices of the people at the 2,800-square-metre Singapore History Gallery.

The museum also offers interesting bits of cultural history through the prisms of fashion, film and *wayang**, photography, and (yes!) food. You might also want to check out the museum for its regular screenings of world cinema in the basement Gallery Theatre and the special exhibitions.

WORTH A TRIP

To discover Singapore's history through fashion, film, photography and food.

For museum events such as special exhibitions and world cinema screenings.

TAKE A TRIP IN TIME AT THE BATTLE BOX

WORTH A TRIP

To witness a reenactment of the British surrender to the Japanese in 1942.

While Chinatown and other ethnic enclaves are a celebration of Singapore's diversity and life, the Battle Box represents the island's bleakest time under Japanese rule as, Syonan-to*, which means the "Island of the Light of the South".

The Battle Box, originally part of the Malaya Command Headquarters in World War II, was notable for its part in the British surrender to the Japanese on 15 February 1942. Thereafter, it was the time when the Japanese created the Sook Ching, or "purge through purification", to remove anti-Japanese elements. This claimed between 25,000 and 50,000 lives in Singapore and Malaya.

Within the Battle Box is the surrender scene of the British to the Japanese, with audio and video effects and animatronics. All you need to do is to hush and listen. Perhaps you might just hear war tales from old ghosts.

DISCOVER THE SINGAPORE PHILATELIC MUSEUM

DID YOU

Discover rare and unusual stamps from Singapore's early history?

Tucked away at the corner of Coleman Street and Hill Street is a nondescript museum that's dedicated to stamps (yes, that scrip of colourful paper pasted on the top right-hand corner of any letter).

Despite its geeky overtones, the Singapore Philatelic Museum is a fun place to learn about stamps. Their permanent galleries are colour-coded into Orange which shows how stamps are used to explore science, technology and history; Purple which focuses on stamp production; and Green, a collection from famous stamp-collectors. Do look out for their roving stamp exhibitions which have quirky themes such as comic characters (think Iron Man) or topical events like Formula One races.

CATCH THE ASIAN ART BUG AT SINGAPORE ART MUSEUM

DID YOU

Discover a new contemporary Southeast Asian artist?

Catch up with the latest in new media, film, and sound art at 8QSAM?

There's been a surge in artistic activity around Singapore past Y2K, with the opening of the School of the Arts, the launching of the Singapore Biennale, and a general air of enhanced art appreciation on the street. Singapore is upping its game in the arts...

... So if you're interested in new directions in Southeast Asian art or the collections of contemporary Asian artists, the Singapore Art Museum promises a worthy trip. No dusty relics here, just 7000 or more art pieces by groups as diverse as the pioneer Nanyang artists, the contemporary Chinese painters, and regional Indonesian and Vietnamese artists.

You might like SAM's latest gallery extension, the 8QSAM, where the works of filmmakers, video, new media and sound artists get their due showcase alongside painters, sculptors and photographers, bringing you closer to the pulse of contemporary art in the eclectic 21st century.

CATCH THE ASIAN ART BUG AT SINGAPORE ART MUSEUM

DID YOU KNOW?

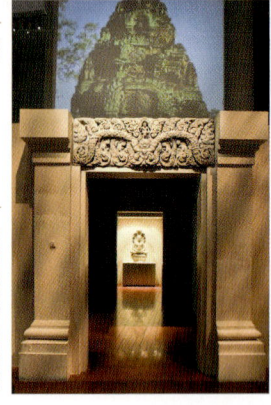

ACM displays over 1300 artefacts, with the oldest pieces dating back to 600BC?

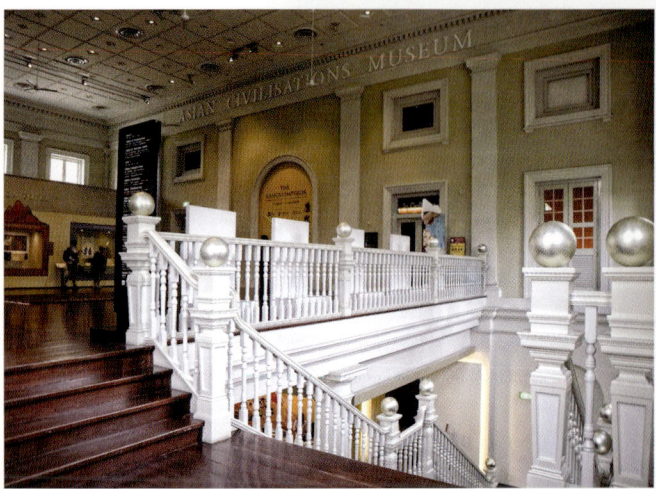

DISCOVER ASIAN HISTORY AT THE ASIAN CIVILISATIONS MUSEUM

With its connections to the rest of Asia and an efficient infrastructure, Singapore is often a gateway to the region. It almost feels natural that Singapore is also home to one of the foremost museums in Asia dedicated to the material history of pan-Asian cultures and civilisations.

Enter the Asian Civilisations Museum (ACM) which traces the history of cultures in China, South Asia, West Asia, and Southeast Asia. With three levels and over 11 galleries, there's much to see and do with the interactive ExplorAsian zones and in-gallery videos.

And the best part of the museum? The fascinating 1300 artefacts on display. The impressive collection includes religious Buddhist and Hindu items, porcelain pieces from the Ming and Qing dynasty and textiles from Southeast Asia. We hear artefacts date back to as early as 600 BC.

RECOMMENDED FOR

Learning who the Peranakans were, their culture and costumes

DISCOVER ETHNIC FLAVOURS AT THE PERANAKAN MUSEUM

Behold the Peranakans! This group of people – descended from foreign traders and local women – took the best and tastiest of their parent cultures to blend into a unique stew of *bibiks**, *babas**, and *kueh pie ties**.

But it's hard to pick out a Peranakan, unless they're sashaying about in their *nonya kebayas** or bantering in Patois. That's why The Peranankan Museum is such a gem. Housed in a refurbished school building, this museum is dedicated to all things Peranakan – from the tassles on a wedding bed to their elaborate costumes. So if you can't find yourself a Peranakan person, well then this is the next best way to learn about them.

TAKE A LEISURELY STROLL AT FORT CANNING PARK

Want a quick escape from the city? Fort Canning Park is all lush greenery and mere minutes away from Dhoby Ghaut and the City Hall area. A caveat: you'll have to go uphill to explore this 60-metre-tall . The extra effort is worth it, however: the signposts are many as you learn about Fort Canning Park's multiple roles in Singapore's history due to its central location and slight elevation.

In the 14th century, few dared to enter this area: the park's old Malay moniker is Bukit Larangan (or Forbidden Hill) and the hill is believed to have housed Malay kings of old. A leisurely stroll around Fort Canning Park brings new discoveries. Singapore's first experimental spice garden? Check. The tomb of ancient kings? Check. Watch out for the old fort walls which protected Singapore from attacks and the curious array of tropical trees and flora.

DID YOU KNOW?

Fort Canning Hill played many roles in Singapore's history, housing palaces of old Malay kings to old British Forts protecting Singapore from attacks.

CATCH EXPERIMENTAL ART AT THE SUBSTATION

The Substation may not be a museum or a large-scale arts venue, but this shop house in the colonial district is the breeding ground for the local arts collective. Founded in 1990 by one of Singapore's cultural greats, the late Kuo Pao Kun, the Substation is where the dreamers and the eccentrics dare to play.

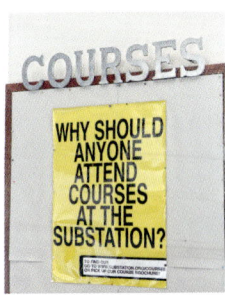

Independent and experimental art events abound here for those interested to see what's brewing on the ground. Poke your head here on the first Monday of the month for First Take, a screening of short films by aspiring local filmmakers. The Substation nurtures a select list of Associate Artists across film, performing and visual arts, so there are regular showcases of the artists' work. The Substation hosts a diverse range of events; take for example, fortnightly book readings of local plays, film festivals and gigs by local and regional bands. We recommend checking www.substation.org for the latest happenings.

REMEMBER TO

Look up the latest events at www.substation.org.

GRAB A SINGAPORE SLING AT RAFFLES HOTEL

REMEMBER TO

Request for a shaken version of the Singapore Sling.

When in Singapore, grab the drink that put us on the map.

This sweet, pink and packed-with-a-wallop gin cocktail was first shaken in 1915 by Mr Ngiam Tong Boon at the Raffles Hotel. In fact, one should have it at the hotel's Long Bar where fans turn lazily like in colonial days of yore.

But no one's sure if it's the original Singapore Sling that's poured from behind the counter as Mr Ngiam's recipe for success was lost through time. The current concoction is reportedly based on the recipe by Ngiam Dee Suan, the creator's nephew, as unearthed by then manager of Raffles Hotel, Roberto Pregarz.

Whatever the case, it's worth a sip and slurp of the foamy Sling. Remember to get the bartenders to shake it, and if it helps – call for a "Gin Sling".

GET ON TOP OF THE CITY AT ROOFTOP BARS

WORTH A TRIP

For a bird's eye view of the Singapore city skyline and the Marina Bay area

These rooftop bars are some of the hottest seats in town. Located in the colonial district, the word on the street is great views, great location. Where else can you take in the sparkling sights of the Marina Bay Sands hotel, the Singapore Flyer and the Fullerton Bay area while sipping on your cocktail?

Orgo at the Esplanade – Theatres on the Bay rooftop gets top marks for its glass-house settings facing the Marina waterfront, and unusual cocktails mixed from "organic" ingredients such as fresh watermelons, peaches and rose. Popular with young executives, Loof at Odeon Towers is chilled-out and chic where no two seats are alike. New Asia Bar is the king of the pack, at 71-storeys above ground at the Swissôtel The Stamford. Pop a bottle of champagne for a classy night out while the joint spins house, funk and Motown music.

DID YOU

Soak in the atmosphere of this old church from 1892?

HAVE ROMANCE
ON THE LAWN AT CHIJMES

This old church comes with an amazing sunken courtyard, and it's got history to boot as it has been around since 1892. So instead of bulldozing Chijmes, we've retrofitted it, turning it into a wine and dine complex for the well-heeled.

Come nightfall, tables crowd the sunken courtyard as thirsty and hungry executives jostle for a pint of beer and ribs at Le Baroque or Table 108 for Asian food with the occasional jazz sessions thrown in for good measure.

That's for fun. For romance, it is best seen to on the quiet lawn under twinkling stars and Gothic church steeples. After all, tête à tête amoureux are best whispered and not shouted. Some of the better places on the lawn include Esmirada for Mediterranean kebabs, or Insomnia Bar & Restaurant, a 24-hour bar/restaurant where dancing the night away after dinner is always welcome.

TAKE A RIDE IN A TRISHAW

DID YOU

Smile at onlooking passersby while riding in your trishaw?

Forget the train and buses – why not take a trishaw ride for a leisurely spin around the colonial district? Trishaws were the main mode of transportation in 1940s Singapore, so a ride is akin to feeling the pace of life in the early 20th century.

These friendly trishaw drivers will pedal-ride you through rain or shine and the city traffic. Simply hop on the seats at the side of the bicycle and pull on the hood to shade yourself from the sun.

Some of the trishaws come with loud radios blaring nostalgic tunes or flashing lights for a festive atmosphere. Riding a trishaw through town will loudly announce your status as a tourist, but forget the onlooking passersby – we say bask in the glory and soak in the sights.

(P.S: If you're hitching a ride from a vendor hawking his services on the street, remember to bargain for a good price.)

SEE A SHOW AT THE ESPLANADE

WATCH OUT FOR

One of Esplanade's highly-anticipated festivals such as the Mosaic Music Festival and the Singapore Arts Festival

Mark your calendars when in town, folks. Singapore's premier arts venue, Esplanade – Theatres on the Bay, has developed a tight schedule of performances throughout the year.

The Singapore Arts Festival returns every mid-year with stellar troupes of international and local dance, theatre and music groups. Musicians from every genre (jazz, world-music, folk, rock, funk and indie) pack the theatres for the highly-anticipated annual Mosaic Music Festival. The Huayi Chinese Festival is an extravaganza of traditional and contemporary Chinese art; while the alternative music event, Baybeats, offers free performances by up-and-coming bands on the waterfront.

With world-class facilities, an accessible location, and a cacophony of food and beverage joints along the waterfront, there's no better place to indulge your inner arts-bug. For details on upcoming shows and ticket prices, visit www.esplanade.com.

COLONIAL DISTRICT

GO FOR LATE NIGHT SUPPER AT MAKANSUTRA GLUTTONS BAY

DID YOU

Dip toasty bread sticks into creamy *kaya**?

Discover what carrot cake means, Singapore-style?

Sweat in the Singapore heat over a plate of spicy *sambal** stingray?

There's no lack of good food in Singapore past midnight. When the choosing gets tough, Makansutra Gluttons Bay is a shoo-in for a late night supper.

The stalls at Gluttons Bay have been handpicked by Singapore's guru of hawker food, K. F. Seetoh. What awaits is the crème de la crème of local goodies, with an atmosphere to boot (read: an *al fresco* setting under giant umbrellas, amid balmy sea breezes and a view of the Marina Bay skyline).

Go gaga over Soon Lee's *char kway teow**, fried Hokkien noodles and or *luak**. The *Roti Kaya** Fondue, (toasted bread sticks dipped in *kaya**) from Gluttons Bar & Sweet Spot will satisfy any sweet tooth. Tantalising *satay** sticks from Alhambra Padang Satay and crispy fried carrot cake from Huat Huat are perennial favourites. If you're up for a more intense experience, Boon Tat Seafood whips up a mean barbequed stingray with a powerful *sambal** sauce.

All stalls stay open till 2am (Mondays to Thursdays), 3am (Fridays to Saturdays) and 1am (Sundays).

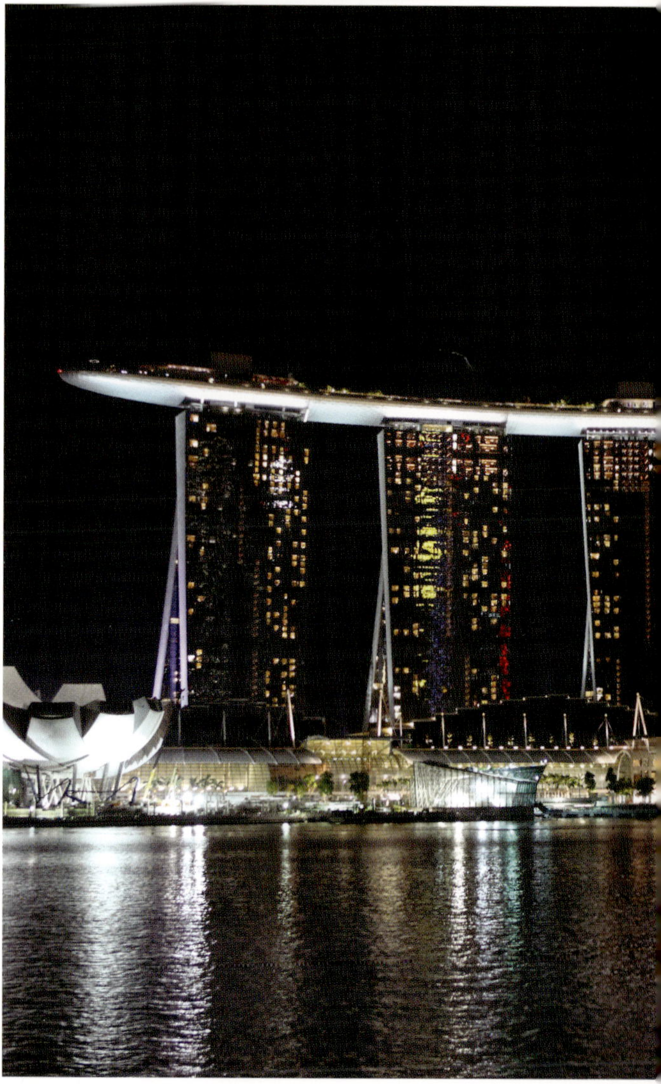

MARINA BAY / FULLERTON HERITAGE

In the 1990s, the Marina Bay and the Fullerton Heritage precincts were sleepy locales, with little activity, upmarket restaurants, or fashion-forward architecture. In the new millennium, they became the focal sites for the local government's game plan towards transforming Singapore into a "global city". The reason: their proximity to the city centre, and a blessed waterfront location.

Look what a difference a decade makes. The plans for re-invention have kicked in, spawning an artfully programmed series of urban spaces by the waterfront that are as far-sighted as they are ingenious. The garden city's most visible icon, the Marina Bay Sands Integrated Resorts designed by Safdie Architects, brings to town a number of firsts: first sky park, first Art-Science Museum, and first city check-in service. The Fullerton Heritage district has revitalised its historical buildings – One Fullerton, Clifford Pier, Customs House, The Fullerton Bay Hotel Singapore, The Fullerton Waterboat House and The Fullerton Hotel Singapore – with an infusion of upscale dining, retail and entertainment options.

And it's not just about the shopping and dining – the Marina Bay and Fullerton Heritage areas also boast spacious promenades which ease the sense of the city's urban density. A 3.5km waterfront promenade links the Marina Centre and Bay front areas, while the Gardens by the Bay, a series of three major parks completed in 2011, offer both locals and tourist more options for enjoying sports and nature.

THE SPOTS

___1 CLIFFORD PIER
80 Collyer Quay, Clifford Pier
Singapore 049326
www.thefullertonheritage.com

___2 CUSTOMS HOUSE
No. 70 Collyer Quay, Singapore 049323
www.thefullertonheritage.com

___3 FORLINO
One Fullerton Road #02-06
One Fullerton, Singapore 049213
Tel: 6877 6995
www.forlino.com

___4 LANTERN
No. 80 Collyer Quay, Rooftop
The Fullerton Bay Hotel Singapore
Singapore 049326
Tel: 6597 5299
www.fullertonbayhotel.com

___5 LE SAINT JULIEN
No. 3 Fullerton Road #02-01
The Fullerton Waterboat House
Singapore 049215
Tel: 6534 5947
www.julienbompard.com

___6 ONE FULLERTON
One Fullerton Road, Singapore 049213
thefullertonheritage.com

___7 KINKI RESTAURANT & BAR
No. 70 Collyer Quay #02-02
Customs House, Singapore 049323
Tel: 6533 3471
www.kinki.com.sg

___8 MARINA BARRAGE
8 Marina Gardens Drive
Singapore 018951
Tel: 6514 5959
www.pub.gov.sg/marina

___9 MARINA BAY SANDS
INTEGRATED RESORT
10 Bayfront Avenue, Singapore 018956
Tel: 6688 8868
www.marinabaysands.com

___10 ONE ON THE BUND
80 Collyer Quay, Clifford Pier
Singapore 049326
Tel: 6221 0004
www.wws.com.hk

___11 SINGAPORE FLYER
30 Raffles Avenue #01-07, Singapore 039803
Tel: 6734 8829
www.singaporeflyer.com

___12 SINGAPORE FORMULA ONE
www.singaporegp.sg

___13 THE BUTTER FACTORY
No. 80 Collyer Quay, Singapore 049326
Tel: 6333 8388
www.fullertonbayhotel.com

___14 THE FULLERTON BAY
HOTEL SINGAPORE
No. 80 Collyer Quay, Singapore 049326
Tel: 6333 8388
www.fullertonbayhotel.com

___15 THE FULLERTON HOTEL SINGAPORE
1 Fullerton Square, Singapore 049178
Tel: 6733 8388
www.fullertonhotel.com

___16 THE FULLERTON WATERBOAT HOUSE
No. 3 Fullerton Road, Singapore 049215
thefullertonheritage.com

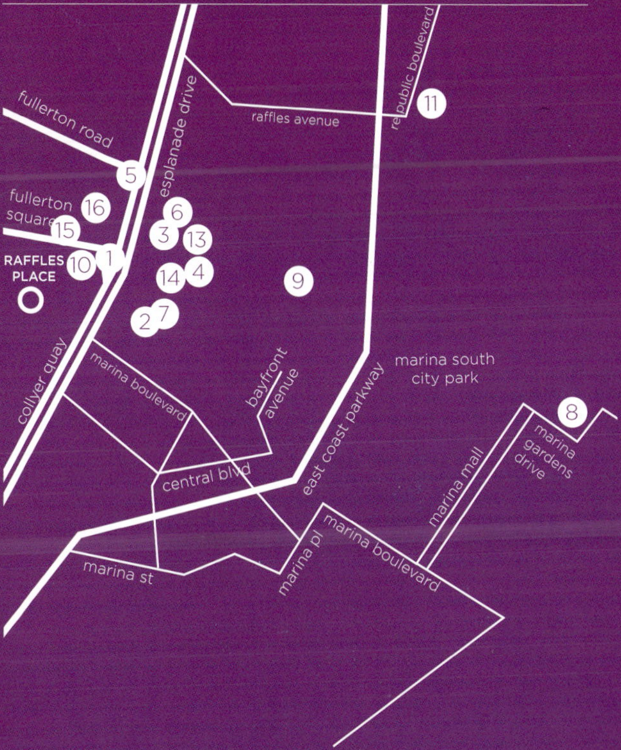
fullerton road
esplanade drive
raffles avenue
republic boulevard
fullerton square
RAFFLES PLACE
collyer quay
marina boulevard
bayfront avenue
east coast parkway
marina south city park
central blvd
marina gardens drive
marina mall
marina pl
marina boulevard
marina st
1
2
3
4
5
6
7
8
9
10
11
13
14
15
16

DID YOU

Have a picnic on the green roof of the Marina Barrage?

ENJOY THE WATER VIEWS AT MARINA BARRAGE

On any weekend, the Marina Barrage is full of flying kites, and kids running on the greenery of this concrete spiral. But did you know that this concrete spiral is actually a 350-metre-wide dam that keeps out the seawater?

Built in 2008, the Marina Barrage, built across the mouth of the Marina Bay, effectively divided the sea to create a freshwater reservoir within the city! In addition to providing much needed water to Singaporeans, the Marina Barrage is also a haunt for sea sports lovers, as you can rent *kayaks** to paddle on the reservoir, windsurf, and boat.

If you're not inclined to head out to sea, the central courtyard's water playground lets both young and old go wet and wild. Otherwise, just pack a picnic basket, and enjoy the water views on the green roof of the Marina Barrage. And if you look into the distance, you can make out the Singapore Flyer against the Marina Bay Sands Integrated Resort.

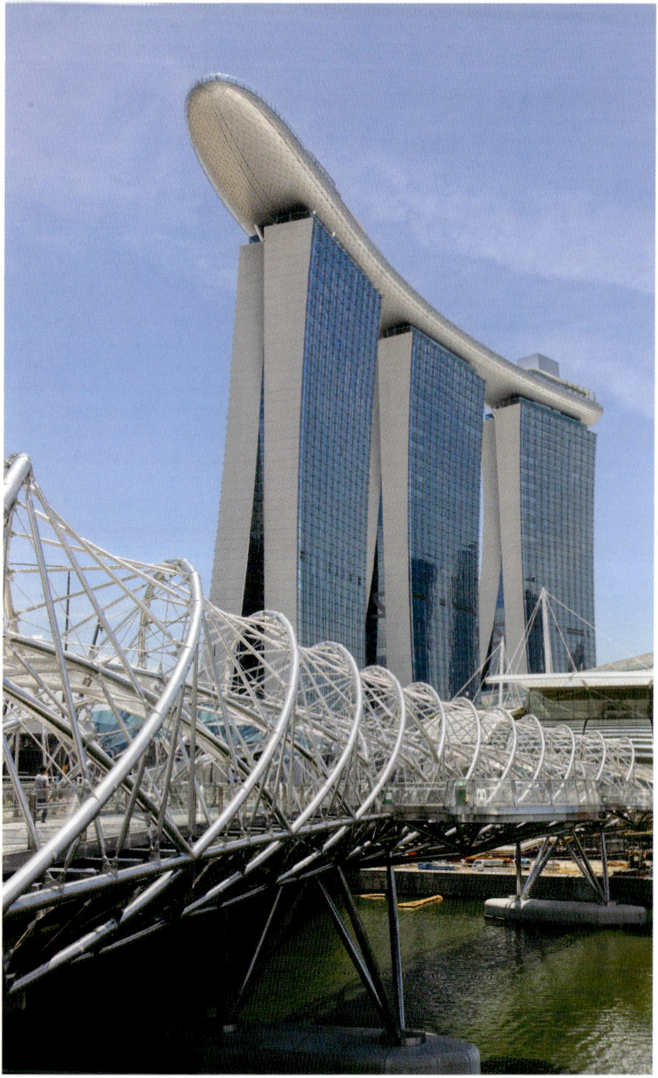

BE AWED BY THE MARINA BAY SANDS INTEGRATED RESORT

DID YOU

Go up to the Sands SkyPark and marvel at the infinity pool?

The glamour of Vegas, the architectural prowess of Chicago, and a touch of the Sydney Harbour: all these factors, merged with the virtues of the Garden City, create the magic that is the Marina Bay Sands Integrated Resort.

Marina Bay Sands has all the features of a mega-entertainment destination and more – like branded stores, an Art-Science museum, hot night clubs, theatres and a melting pot of restaurants helmed by seven world-class celebrity chefs, including The Sky on 57 by Singapore's most celebrated chef, Justin Quek.

At night, head up to the Sands SkyPark, located on the top level of the hotel, for a breathtaking view of Singapore, and the much-famed infinity pool (just don't look down). And if your fingers are peckish for cards or dice, there's always the Marina Bay Sands casino, where fortunes are made (and broken) with a roll of the dice.

PARTY AT THE BUTTER FACTORY

DID YOU

Take your pick from Fash, the electro-friendly room, or Bump, for hip hop favorites?

The Butter Factory has been out on a singular mission: to spread the gospel of fun. At the Butter Factory, do what the regulars do – dance till your legs turn to butter.

The club is known for spinning a thumping party blend of hip hop and R&B, so check in at the 8,000 square feet party space at One Fullerton to find out what the hype is all about.

It's never a dull moment inside the Butter Factory: the interiors are loud and madcap with bodacious graphics, psychedelic prints, and oddball characters looming at every corner.

Party people, take your pick from two main dance floors – Fash, spins electro-friendly ditties, while Bump is where the hip-hop fanatics get their fix of bump and grind.

FLY THE SINGAPORE FLYER

DID YOU

Take a river taxi to the Singapore Flyer?

What's 30 metres taller than the London Eye and gets a bird's eye view of the Singapore city scape? Enter the Singapore Flyer, a 165-metre-tall observation wheel, which sits on prime real estate along the Marina Bay front.

There's something magical about being in a capsule, and watching the sun go down in the garden city. For those looking to indulge, think dining in the skies – the Singapore Flyer offers a 3-course fine-dining dinner menu to be had over a slow one-hour rotation.

Otherwise, the Singapore Flyer is family friendly as kids get a Kid's Fun Pack; and also interestingly, *feng shui** friendly. Trivia buffs may find the *feng shui** audio guides fascinating as a Chinese geomancer explains the various *feng shui** aspects of notable buildings across the city.

Visitors have been loving the river taxis which bring you along the Singapore river to the Flyer. Book via one of these operators: Singapore River Cruises & Leisure and DUCKtours.

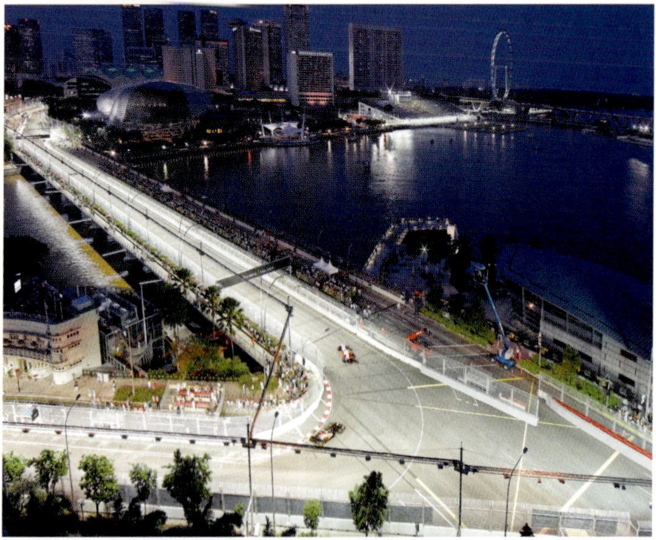

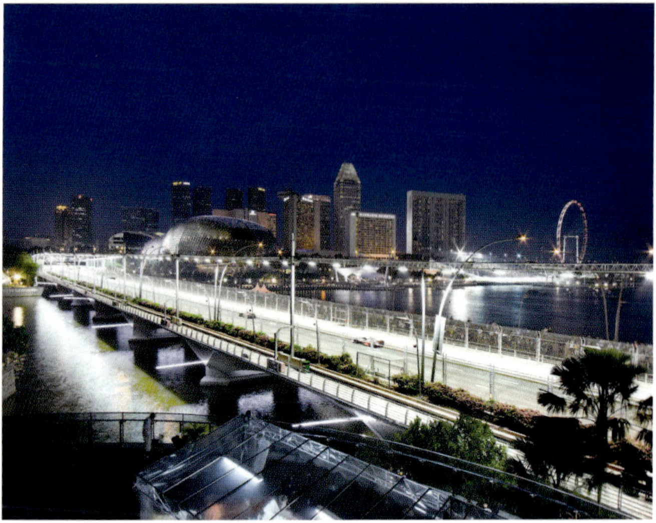

CATCH THE SINGAPORE FORMULA ONE NIGHT RACE

DID YOU

Watch for updates on the upcoming Formula One Night Race at www.singaporegp.sg?

Mark your calendars: the Singapore Formula One Night Race is one of most anticipated Grand Prix on the calendar. It's when the street lights are pumped up, the roads around Marina Bay and the colonial district are transformed into wide race circuits, all ready to become the stunning backdrop where the racers vie for top prize.

The Formula One Night Race tickets are hot property, and it's not just at the race benches where you'll feel the buzz of speeding cars. The organisers have upped their game by bringing in numerous headlining entertainment acts; past years have seen the likes of Mariah Carey, Missy Elliot, the Backstreet Boys and Beyonce. All psyched? Watch out for updates on the upcoming Formula One Night Race at www.singaporegp.sg (including announcements for how long Singapore will host this highly-anticipated event).

WINE AND DINE AT THE FULLERTON HERITAGE

Put on your best threads: you're having dinner at one of the city's finest dining destinations, a stretch of upscale restaurants in the Fullerton Heritage district. Take your pick from the area's historic buildings: the Fullerton Waterboat House, One Fullerton, Clifford Pier, The Fullerton Bay Hotel Singapore, and Customs House.

There's One on the Bund, a contemporary Chinese restaurant in Clifford Pier, a building once frequented by ferries operating to Singapore's southern islands. Kinki Restaurant & Bar is good for avant-garde sushi and sake martinis and is located in Customs House, a building from which police patrolled the waters. The Fullerton Waterboat House used to supply water, but now it is home to Le Saint Julien, great for Foie gras, smoked salmon and Oscietra Caviar dressing with vodka cream.

Go Italian at Forlino with beef carpaccio and angel hair pasta at One Fullerton. And when you're ready to bring on the champagne, The Fullerton Bay Hotel ups the luxe factor with Lantern, a rooftop bar.

1.3. Customs House
2. One on the Bund 4. Kinki Restaurant + Bar 5. Lantern

2

DID YOU

Dine at one of the Fullerton Heritage's historic buildings?

3

4

5

WINE AND DINE AT THE FULLERTON HERITAGE

211

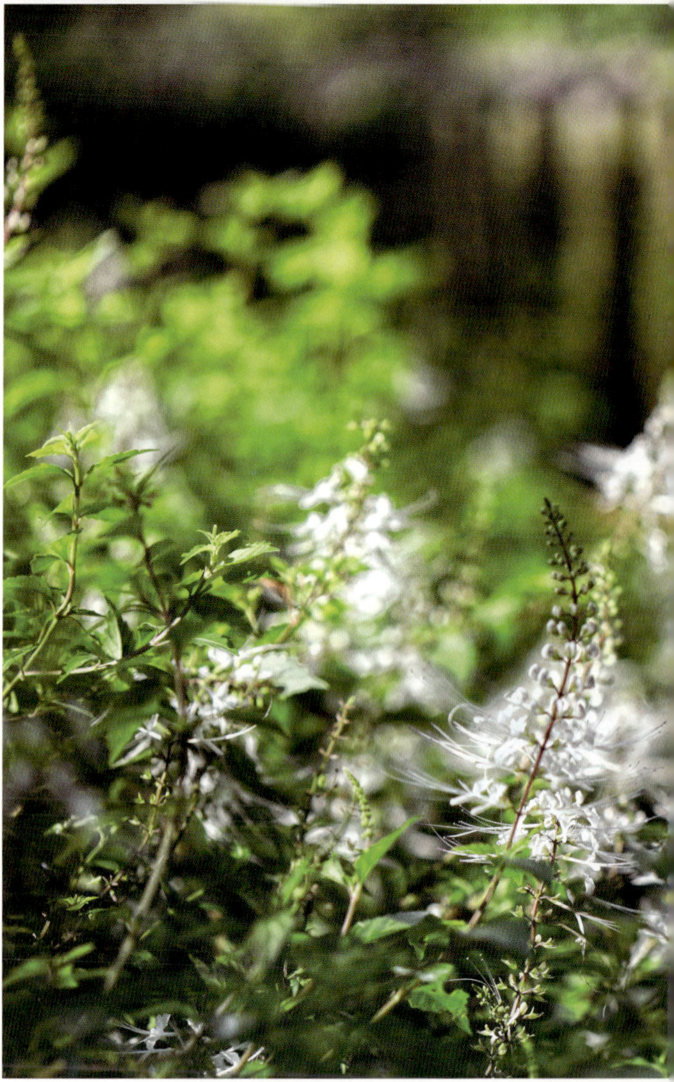

DEMPSEY HILL/
HOLLAND VILLAGE

There's no lack of food options in Singapore, from street level hawkers to restaurant chains, and up-scale fine dining. Just short drives away from Orchard Road, the powerhouse food and beverage enclaves of Dempsey Hill and Holland Village, however, have a particular hook on urbanites and the expatriate community. Read: a bevy of epicurean restaurants, a laidback vibe and lifestyle stores make Dempsey Hill and Holland Village hot spots for wining and dining.

You've got to a hitch a cab to get to Dempsey Hill; expect your cab driver to meander through narrow roads tucked within forestry to find your restaurant. Well, that's all part of the area's charm. Dempsey Hill was once the home to former British military barracks, and the Central Manpower Base of Singapore, while antique furniture stores populated the blocks in the 1990s. Now, you can be privy to the lost-in-time, tucked-away atmosphere at Dempsey Hill's trendy restaurants. The nearby Phoenix Park hideout down Tanglin Road adopts a similar concept, with a bevy of food and beverage and lifestyle joints set in black and white colonial blocks.

Holland Village, a neighbourhood near Buona Vista MRT, has long been popular with expats with its eateries and smattering of lifestyle stores. Lorong Mambong remains Holland Village's epicentre, home to stalwarts like live-music watering hole Wala Wala, ice cream joints and a number of cafes. Spend a pleasurable afternoon combing the art galleries and home furnishings stores at Holland Village Shopping Centre, or walk across to Jalan Merah Saga, where you'll find a mix of specialty kitchen and baking stores, gourmet food outlets and lovely restaurants galore. We say bring on the wine.

THE SPOTS

___ 1 211 ROOF TERRACE CAFÉ
211 Holland Avenue #04-01
Holland Road Shopping Centre
Singapore 278967
Tel: 6462 6194
www.cafe211.com.sg

___ 2 ANGIE'S HANDMADE FASHION
211 Holland Avenue #02-08
Holland Road Shopping Centre
Singapore 278967

___ 3 BARRACKS CAFÉ
8D Dempsey Road, Singapore 249672
Tel: 6475 7787
www.dempseyhouse.com

___ 4 BEAUTY EMPORIUM
8D Dempsey Road, Level 2
Singapore 249672
Tel: 6479 0070 (spa esprit and Mask); 6475 7020 (Browhaus); 6475 7833 (Strip)
www.dempseyhouse.com

___ 5 BISTRO PETIT SALUT
44 Jalan Merah Saga #01-54
Chip Bee Gardens, Singapore 278116
T: 6474 9788
ww.aupetitsalut.com/bps/aboutus.html

___ 6 CAMP BAR
8D Dempsey Road
Singapore 249672
Tel: 6475 7787
www.dempseyhouse.com

___ 7 CAFÉ HACIENDA
13A Dempsey Road, Singapore 249674
Tel: 6476 2922
haciendaconcepts.wordpress.com/cafe-hacienda

___ 8 D'ARTIST GALLERY
211 Holland Avenue #03-24
Holland Road Shopping Centre
Singapore 278967

___ 9 ESPANA LINE
211 Holland Avenue #02-15
Holland Road Shopping Centre
Singapore 278967
Tel: 6466 4198

___ 10 FRAMING ANGIE
211 Holland Avenue #03-02
Holland Road Shopping Centre
Singapore 278967

___ 11 GASTRONOMIA
43 Jalan Merah Saga #01-74
Chip Bee Gardens, Singapore 278115
Tel: 6475 1323
www.dapaolo.com.sg

___ 12 HARRY'S @ DEMPSEY HILL
Blk 11 Dempsey Road #01-17A
Singapore 247673
Tel: 6471 9018; 6471 9019
www.harrys.com.sg

___ 13 HOLLAND ROAD SHOPPING CENTRE
211 Holland Avenue, Singapore 278967

14 LA TERRAZZA
44 Jalan Merah Saga #01-56
Chip Bee Gardens, Singapore 278116
Tel: 6476 1332
www.dapaolo.com.sg

15 LIM'S ART AND LIVING
211 Holland Avenue #02-01
Holland Road Shopping Centre
Singapore 278967
Tel: 6467 1300

16 MICHELANGELO'S RESTAURANT
Blk 44 Jalan Merah Saga #01-60
Chip Bee Gardens, Singapore 278116
Tel: 6475 9069
www.michelangelos.com.sg

17 ORIGINAL SIN
Blk 43 Jalan Merah Saga #01-62
Chip Bee Gardens, Singapore 278115
Tel: 6475 5605
www.originalsin.com.sg

18 PIZZA BAR
44 Jalan Merah Saga #01-46
Singapore 278116
Tel: 6479 6059
www.dapaolo.com.sg

19 PRO-FIT INSTITUTE
316 Tanglin Road #02-01/02
Phoenix Park, Singapore 247978
Tel: 6887 3574
www.profit.com.sg

20 PS.CAFÉ @ HARDING
28B Harding Road, Singapore 249549
Tel: 9070 8782
www.pscafe.sg

21 REDDOT BREWHOUSE
25A Dempsey Road #01-01
Singapore 249697
Tel: 6475 0500
www.reddotbrewhouse.com.sg

22 SPRUCE
320 Tanglin Rd, Phoenix Park
Singapore 247980
Tel: 6836 5528
www.spruce.com.sg

23 THE DAILY SCOOP
43 Jalan Merah Saga #01-78
Chip Bee Gardens, Singapore 278115
Tel: 6475 3128
thedailyscoop.com.sg

24 THE WHITE RABBIT
39C Harding Road, Singapore 249541
Tel: 6473 9975
www.thewhiterabbit.com.sg

25 TIPPLING CLUB
8D Dempsey Road, Singapore 249672
Tel: 6475 2217
www.tipplingclub.com

26 VERITA ADVANCED WELLNESS
308 Tanglin Road, Phoenix Park
Singapore 247974
Tel: 6737 2377
www.veritaadvancedwellness.com

219

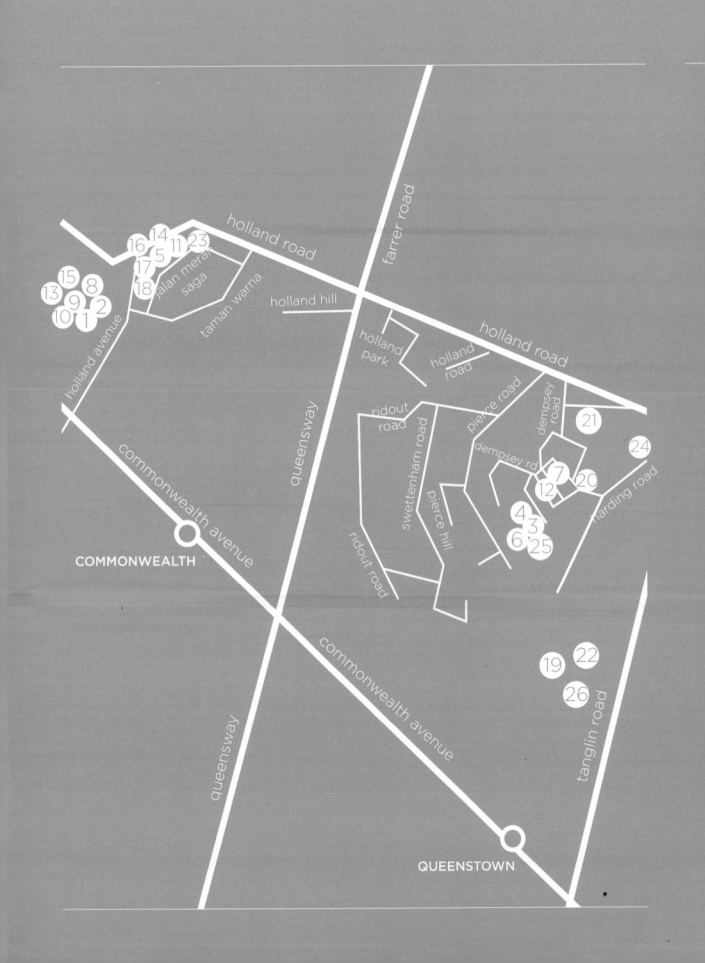

ENJOY SUNDAY BRUNCH AT DEMPSEY HILL

It's a lazy Sunday morning, and you've already missed breakfast. Hop over to Dempsey Hill, where a slew of trendy restaurants are turning Sunday brunch into the *It* meal of the day. A caveat: prices aren't cheap, and hitching a taxi here is a necessity. But take heart: Dempsey Hill's undisputed chilled-out atmosphere, and food artistry are to be experienced.

P.S. Café will grab you with its lush, green surroundings. The best spots are along the outdoor terrace, where relaxing conversations occur over coffee, and epicurean picks, from the *wagyu*-beef burger, to the truffle fries, and perfectly executed poached eggs. Thou shall be awed by the killer interiors at The White Rabbit, an old chapel turned hip restaurant. Its menu touts comfort European fare, to be enjoyed amidst the joint's high ceilings and stained glass windows.

The "council of foodies" over at Barracks Café have "elected" an extensive menu to guarantee you some Sunday brunch flights of fancy. Now, will it be seven-layer pancakes, skinny pizzas or old-fashioned American sliders? For the mother of all brunches, Tippling Club, known for its molecular gastronomy creations, offers a several course brunch degustation menu. If a Sunday brunch isn't enough, die-hard breakfast fans can head to Café Hacienda, which offers breakfast all-day, every-day in a relaxed, low-key environment.

1. P.S. Café
2. Barracks at House
3.4. The White Rabbit

YOU'LL LOVE

Sipping a latte amidst Dempsey Hill's lush green surroundings

ENJOY SUNDAY BRUNCH AT DEMPSEY HILL

221

GET A BEAUTY FIX AT HOUSE'S BEAUTY EMPORIUM

Staying beautiful is all about maintenance and HOUSE's Beauty Emporium gets this. That's why this emporium has whipped together a host of beauty services and products under one roof. When in town, this is the place to go to to keep up with your regular beauty fixes.

The Beauty Emporium is styled like a gourmet supermarket where you pick up well-known beauty brands with yellow mini-trolleys. The idea is to get customers to see, touch and test the products while browsing the aisles. The store stocks high-end beauty brands, such as New York City's Malin + Goetz, UK's Ren, and organic skincare brand Ilsci.

You can also select beauty services *a la carte*: there are the Brazilian waxes by Strip; get your brows trimmed at Browhaus; or look your radiant best with one of Mask's facials. HOUSE's Beauty Emporium likes a bit of fun, so even treatments are given quirky titles. Case in point: spa esprit, HOUSE Beauty Emporium's in-house spa, offers a Cheeky Chai Detox Massage and a Vampirella Wrap.

DON'T MISS

Picking up high-end beauty brands with your trolleys at the Beauty Emporium

1. RedDot Brewhouse
2.3. Camp Bar
4.5. Tippling Club

HIT LATE NIGHT BARS AT INTIMATE DEMPSEY HILL

DID YOU

Sample drinks such as the Tiffin Punch, a micro-brewed Monster Green Lager, or a Snows of Kilimanjaro?

There's something about Dempsey Hill that encourages inebriation and making merry till the moon goes down. We might start at Camp Bar for cutting-edge music and a Tiffin Punch; if the night's balmy and sweet, we'd round off at Café Hacienda where it's like being at a lawn party. Summer dresses or bermudas are the norm, and loading up on champagne is mandatory.

But don't miss out on Harry's, the franchise bar that serves up a mean pint of Guinness alongside good live music. Just to be colourful, drink up a micro-brewed Monster Green Lager – made with Spirulina and it's really green – at the RedDot Brewhouse. End your night at Tippling Club which has rocked the local scene with its molecular gastronomy creations – think cocktails with outlandish names (F*** the Subprime or Snows of Kilimanjaro) with the most epicurian ingredients, from roast apple calvados to bittermens mole bitters.

WANDER AROUND HOLLAND ROAD SHOPPING CENTRE

DID YOU

Stroll the hippy wear boutiques and art and craft stores?

Expatriate housewives love Holland Road Shopping Centre for the many Asian art and crafts and antique shops within its three floors.

At any time of the day, the coiffured brigade will deck themselves out at funky jewellery and hippy wear boutiques such as Angie's Handmade Fashion (#02-08) and Espana Line (#02-15). For a touch of class, they'll troll D'Artist Gallery (#03-24) and Framing Angie (#03-02) for artworks to hang, install and display in their homes. But their ultimate goal lies at Lim's Arts and Living (#02-01) where they tappity-tap on colonial furniture, silk cushion covers, and Asian-style home ware. The shop started out in the 1960s selling souvenirs; now it's a smorgasbord of everything for the home.

If you're joining the coiffured brigade for a romp through Holland Road Shopping Centre, you'll do well to remember these words of advice: stay hydrated with Blue Magaritas at 211 Roof Terrace Cafe (#04-01).

WINE, DINE AND RELAX AT CHIP BEE GARDENS

HEAD HERE TO

Enjoy the peaceful surroundings of Chip Bee Gardens at one of its Italian, French or Mediterranean restaurants.

There may be times when the popular Holland Village gets overrun by office workers and feckless youths lounging in sidewalk cafes. Our remedy: cross the road and into Chip Bee Gardens, a quiet neighbourhood for some of the best Italian, French and Mediterranean dining spots.

There's Da Paolo – a triumvirate of La Terrazza, Pizza Bar, and Gastronomia for eat-in risottos, pizzas, or takeaways; you pick. While Bistro Petit Salut offers hearty French food without breaking the bank; carnivores will stray at Original Sin as their portobello mushrooms and other Mediterranean vegetarian dishes are simply irresistible. Need wine? Go gaga at Michelangelo's extensive wine list (over 200 labels); they're served best with the Penne Sambuca. Or sweeten your tongue at The Daily Scoop with fresh ice cream that's made in-house.

Best of all, it's peace away from the slipper-slapping Holland Village crowds.

LIVE WELL AT PHOENIX PARK

WE LIKE

How the Phoenix Park hideout is only minutes away from the main Orchard Road stretch.

Just a stone's throw away from Orchard Road, yet far enough from main street, Phoenix Park is a private pocket of black and white colonial blocks down Tanglin Road. Located opposite the High Commission of Brunei Darussalam, Phoenix Park is still an obscure location if you don't drive, but it's the possibility of 'getting away from the crowds' only minutes away and checking out the area's various service offerings.

Foodies should head straight to Spruce, a restaurant, bar and bakery that's been grabbing attention for its laid-back ambience, lush surroundings and weekend brunches. Health buffs, listen up: Singapore's largest integrated wellness centre, the 17,000 square feet Verita Advanced Wellness Centre is located here. Billed as being at the forefront of the wellness industry, the centre offers services combining natural healing methods and the latest technology. Fitness enthusiasts will find a home at Pro-fit Institute, a gym which emphasises professional personal trainers and solid fitness programmes without the gimmicks and hard-sell.

1.2.5. Spruce
3.4. Verita Advanced Wellness Centre

LIVE WELL AT PHOENIX PARK

229

BUONA VISTA/ ALEXANDRA

Watch out: Singapore's south-western hemisphere may soon be considered a serious lifestyle destination. The area is feeding Singapore's voracious appetite for the next secret enclave. Enter Rochester Park, Portsdown Road and Wessex Estate. These clusters of restaurants and lifestyle stores have sprouted up in little pockets from Buona Vista all the way down to Alexandra. Think generous greenery, wide-open spaces and old British houses and barracks transformed into restaurants, and you'll understand why these emerging spots have captured an enthusiastic audience in land-scarce Singapore.

With its tranquil yet classy setting, Rochester Park is a place to pamper yourself with its number of swanky restaurants offering everything from French cuisine, Szechuan delicacies to fine wines. The Wessex Estate is one of the few places in Singapore that nurtures an artistic community. The various black and white bungalows house art studios – rub shoulders with the artists at the restaurants in the Village Square. Boosting the south-west's credentials for abundant greenery are the Southern Ridges, a series of parks stretching nine kilometres, and HortPark, a innovative gardening and lifestyle hub. Just remember to get there before the crowds.

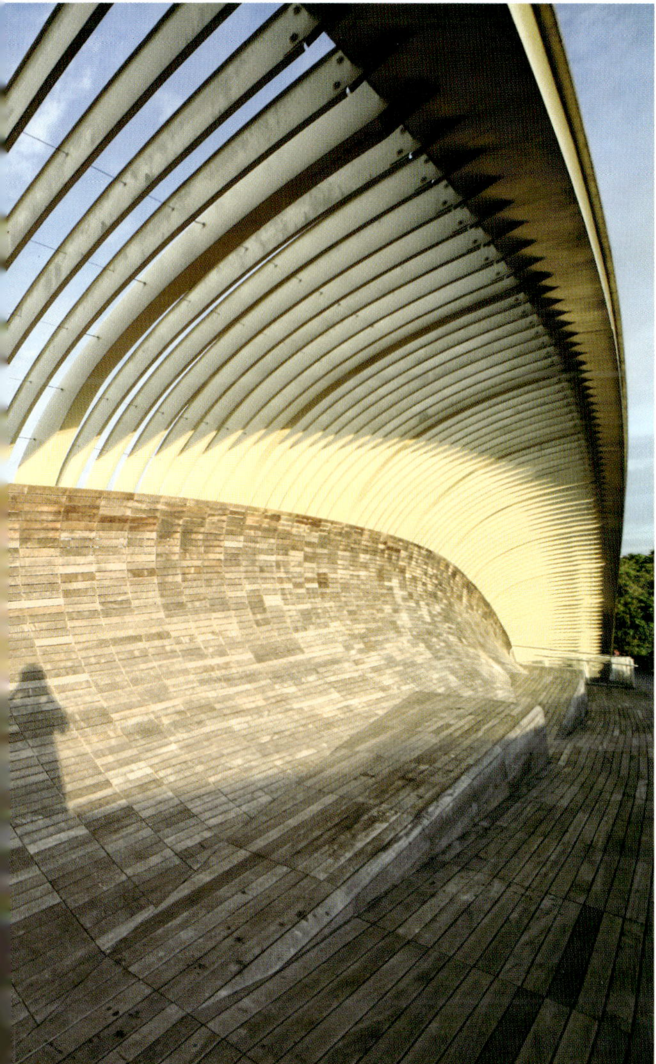

THE SPOTS

__ 1 COLBAR
9A Whitchurch Road, Wessex Estate
Singapore 138839
Tel: 6779 4859

__ 2 D'ART STUDIO
5 Westbourne Road #02-03
Blenheim Court, Singapore 138944
Tel: 6479 7906
www.d-artstudio.com.sg

__ 3 FRINGE BENEFITS
5B Portsdown Road
Wessex Square #01-01
Singapore 139311
fringebenefitsgallery.com

__ 4 GEELEINAN ART GALLERY
Blk 1 Whitchurch Road #02-03
Wessex Estate, Singapore 138941
www.geeleinan.com.sg

__ 5 GRAZE
4 Rochester Park Singapore 139215
Tel: 6775 9000
www.graze.com.sg

__ 6 HORTPARK
33 Hyderabad Road, Singapore 119578
Tel: 6471 5601
www.nparks.gov.sg

__ 7 KLEE
5B Portsdown Road #01-04
Wessex Estate, Singapore 139311
Tel: 6479 6911
www.klee.com.sg

__ 8 KRISH
9 Rochester Park, Singapore 139220
Tel: 6779 4644
www.krish.com.sg

__ 9 LABRADOR NATURE RESERVE
Labrador Villa Road, Singapore 119187
www.nparks.gov.sg

__ 10 MIN JIANG
5 Rochester Park, Singapore 139216
Tel: 6774 0122

__ 11 NORTH BORDER BAR AND GRILL
2 Rochester Park, Singapore 139213
Tel: 6777 6618
www.northborder.com.sg

__ 12 PIETRASANTA
5B Portsdown Road #01-03
Singapore 139311
Tel: 6479 9521
www.ristorante-pietrasanta.com

__ 13 THE SOUTHERN RIDGES
From Marang Road, Mount Faber,
Telok Blangah, Alexandra Road,
Hyderabad Road, to South Buona
Vista Road
www.nparks.gov.sg

__ 14 REFLECTIONS AT BUKIT CHANDU
31K Pepys Road, Singapore 118458
Tel: 6375 2510
www.s1942.org.sg/s1942/bukit_chandu/homepage.htm

Map

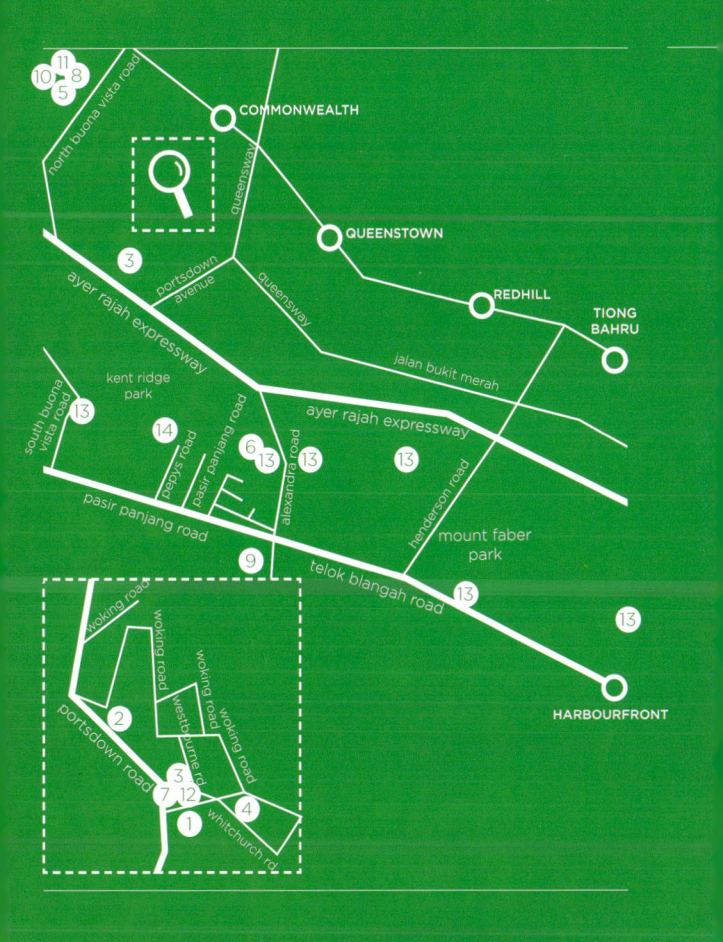

Stations: COMMONWEALTH, QUEENSTOWN, REDHILL, TIONG BAHRU, HARBOURFRONT

Roads: north buona vista road, queensway, portsdown avenue, ayer rajah expressway, jalan bukit merah, south buona vista road, kent ridge park, pepys road, pasir panjang road, alexandra road, henderson road, mount faber park, telok blangah road, woking road, portsdown road, westbourne rd, whitchurch rd

BUONA VISTA/ALEXANDRA

DID YOU

Quaff on British ales and lagers, or chomp on fish and chips in this old British canteen?

GO BACK IN TIME AT COLBAR

The regulars love Colbar for its history. Old timers laze, booze and stretch out on dinky plastic chairs at this wooden shack in the middle of an artist commune. In 1953, it was once a canteen for British soldiers and Colbar served up comfort food – fish and chips or bangers and mash alongside a pint of British ale – to slake their homesickness.

It hasn't changed since then, even as the old Colbar had to be relocated a few hundred metres away from its original location in Jalan Hang Jebat in 2003. The road where Colbar stood was being widened; fortunately, public outcry and numerous petitions fell on sympathetic ears and the authorities relocated it a stone's throw away from the old site. Every brick and plank was moved; what could not be moved was replicated exactly.

Diners and drinkers eat and booze within blue wooden walls that frame chicken wire windows, under a signboard still fresh from the 1950s, and amongst black and white photos from that era. The food's still the same old with fish and chips, and liver chips taking pole position on their ratty menu; quaffing on their stock of British ales and lagers is a must. Go in the evenings when it's cooler and bring mosquito repellent.

WATCH OUT FOR

Open studio season where Wessex Estate's artistic inhabitants invite you into their workspaces.

VISIT ARTIST HIDEAWAYS IN THE WILD AT WESSEX ESTATE

With Wessex Estate's rolling slopes and peaceful atmosphere, it offers more than just a pleasant evening stroll. The estate's many black and white walk-up apartments – once British army officers' abodes in the 1940s – are today artists' studios.

The estate attracted many an artist who turned them into exhibition spaces and studios. Like D'Art Studio, by Dick Lim, a graphic advertising industry veteran who ventured into fine arts; Fringe Benefits which develops artists via workshops and sporadic exhibitions; and Geeleinan Singapore which showcases sculptures and oil paintings by Malaysian Gee Michaud.

The artists' studios might not always be open, but keep an eye out for their infrequent Open Studios (http://sites.google.com/site/wessexarts/Home/2009-event-team/links-to-websites-of-artists) where Wessex Estate's inhabitants welcome one and all into their studios.

DID YOU

Dine in classy restaurants amidst lush greenery?

DINE IN A SECRET GARDEN AT ROCHESTER PARK AND PORTSDOWN ROAD

Expand your dining horizons to Rochester Park and Portsdown Road, where eating amidst natural greenery is the order of the day. The two streets extend off the main North Buona Vista Road and are within minutes from each other. On Portsdown road, go Tuscany with Squid Ink pasta at Pietrasanta but always end the evening with tasty cocktails by Klee.

Most folks know One Rochester for its lush gardens and alcoholic liquid desserts. But alcohol isn't food (at least for most of us), so we'll head to Graze for their Crispy Handrolled Pork Hock, or turn Yankee at North Border Bar and Grill with hearty rib racks. For Asian flavours, Min Jiang at One North makes great Peking Duck, whilst Krish fuses Europe with a touch of India.

1,2. Klee 3. One Rochester

SPEND AFTERNOONS AT THE GARDENS AT HORTPARK

Singapore is often called the Garden City, and HortPark may well be a microcosm for the shining possibilities when gardening, landscaping and plant knowledge are properly harnessed. Not just meant to be gardens for leisure, HortPark is billed as a one-stop lifestyle 23-hectare educational gardening hub, with 21 interestingly themed garden parks.

It's unlikely you'll spend an afternoon here without being inspired to design your own garden. Vertical wall gardens, garden swings and vegetable plots – HortPark has it all. Watch out for the Garden Patch, a series of plots with expressive new garden designs, concepts and products; and the Silver Garden, a fascinating spot where the plants are all gorgeously silver, grey and white hued. For activities such as guided tours and workshops, visit www.nparks.gov.sg.

1.3. Silver Garden 2.6. Garden Patch
4.5. Vertical wall gardens

DID YOU

Get inspired by HortPark's 21 themed garden parks?

HIKE ON THE SOUTHERN RIDGES

Need to stretch your legs? Head down south and onto the Southern Ridges – a nine-kilometre trail that connects Mount Faber, Telok Blangah Hill and Kent Ridge Park in one unbroken stretch.

The trail is broken up into eight distinctive parts, starting with Marang Trail which winds from Habourfront MRT to Mount Faber's Jewel Box; Faber Trail that goes through Faber Park and ends at Henderson Waves, an architectural masterpiece that's a cross between a wave form and a giant's ribs.

Then brush over canopies of trees on the Hilltop Walk and Forest Walk for a bird's eye view of the forest before climbing over Alexandra Arch – a 80-metre long bridge that's designed like an opened leaf – to enter HortPark: a one-stop shop for gardening-related recreational and educational activities. Finish off with a stroll through Kent Ridge Park which ends at Reflections at Bukit Chandu.

For more information, check out NParks website at www.nparks.gov.sg.

DID YOU

Catch sight of twin architectural bridges Henderson Waves and the Alexandra Arch?

Stroll across a canopy of trees on the Hilltop Walk and Forest Walk?

REMEMBER OUR WARTIME DEAD AT REFLECTIONS AT BUKIT CHANDU

The dead speak on Bukit Chandu (Opium Hill), not in some ghostly, paranormal manner but through the multimedia exhibitions of Reflections at Bukit Chandu. This museum commemorates the last and fiercest battle between the Japanese and Malay Regiment soldiers on 15 February 1942. The regiment held the hill for 48 hours against overwhelming odds before they ran out of ammunition and were overrun.

There were no survivors.

The museum's exhibits are poignant reminders of those trying times. Experience the battle with the museum's interpretive and interactive exhibits, and a 10-minute award-winning animated feature with a re-enactment of the battle. For more moving memoirs, there's the Well of Reflections where stark accounts by an old man, child and widow recall how a sergeant, father and husband fought and died on Opium Hill.

DID YOU KNOW?

A fierce battle was fought on 15 February 1942 on Bukit Chandu where Malay Regiment soldiers held out in vain against Japanese troops.

DID YOU KNOW?

The secret tunnels beneath an old British fort used to hide troops during World War II.

EXPLORE SINGAPORE'S 'CU CHI TUNNELS' AT LABRADOR NATURE RESERVE

One park is the same as another – that's until you've been through Labrador Nature Reserve.

Hidden in Labrador Nature Reserve's 10-hectares are historical relics from World War II and the British army, such as the secret tunnels beneath an old fort. They were used to store ammunition and supplies, and hide British troops. One of the tunnels reportedly goes under the sea to Pulau Blakang Mati (aka Sentosa). While that tunnel remains closed, the nature reserve has opened the other tunnels for public perusal and it's worth the jaunt.

In addition, there's a rock (aka Long Ya Men or Dragon's Tooth Gate) that juts out at the park's waterfront edge. It was used by Admiral Cheng Ho to navigate around Singapore's waters. (P.S. the rock's a replica as the original was destroyed by the British to widen the harbour's entrance.).

APPENDIX

Singapore's Unique Eating Places – the Hawker Centre and Kopi tiam

As immigrants moved to Singapore during the British colonial era, they brought with them the traditional cuisines of their homelands. Between 1800 to 1900, street hawkers were the order of the day. Dishes were whipped up out of travelling 'cook shops' – a makeshift kitchen where hawkers sold a meal for a few cents. Street hawker fare was extremely popular with coolies and workers in the 19th century. As Singapore developed, these street hawkers were moved off the streets into hawker centres: organised rows of food stalls, with shelter and communal seating. The local *kopi tiam** or coffee shops evolved from a similar concept. They began as makeshift wooden carts or structures, with a few tables where owners sold drinks to workers in plantations.

Architectural styles of the Singaporean shophouse

The typical shophouse is a two or more storied house which were meant for both commercial and residential use; built from the early 1800s, the design of the shophouse has changed throughout its history resulting in a myriad of styles. Early Style shophouses had the least ornamentation and only one or two windows on the upper floors (1840-1900). The First Transitional shop house possessed two windows and is noted for its simplicity, though with slightly more decoration such as Chinese petals. The most recognisable style is the Late Shophouse Style (1900-1940) with three windows, and highly ornate wall tiles drawing inspiration from Chinese, Malay and European influences. The Second Transitional style forms a bridge between the Late Style period and the Art Deco period with elements of both; the Art Deco period (1930-1960) started to reflect architects' interest in geometric forms, with the ornamentation, such as wall tiles, of the late period largely lost.

Where Singaporeans live: HDB Flats

You'll find these ubiquitous around Singapore's neighbourhoods: high-rise flats, or Housing Development Board (HDB) flats, where most Singaporeans live. At around 710 square kilometres today, Singapore's land scarcity posed unique problems for urban development. When the Republic of Singapore declared its independence from Malaysia in 1965, the ruling party, the People's Action Party, set up the Housing Development Board (HDB) to tackle the issue of housing shortages. The rise of HDB flats, high-rise buildings with relatively similar-sized apartments, provided low-cost housing for the general population while maximising area space. The government has also put in a place a quota system, which requires a certain racial mix within the HDB blocks to promote racial integration. Today, around 85% of Singaporeans live in HDB flats in residential neighbourhoods across Singapore.

PUBLIC HOLIDAYS

Thanks to Singapore's multi-racial, multi-religious society, public holidays are all about inclusiveness and a good dose of understanding about another culture's festivities and practices.

New Year's Day – 1 January
In Singapore, it's all about the countdown ushering in the new year. Countdown parties are held across the country in malls, at beaches, along Orchard Road – basically, everywhere. Various hotspots vie for the crowd's patronage, where partying goes on till dawn.

Chinese New Year – During the months of January or February, according to the Chinese calendar
Chinese around the world celebrate the Lunar New Year, and Singapore is no exception. Chinatown is decked out in festive garb, as families stock up on snacks and goodies to welcome visitors. During this period, the Chinese visit relatives and friends dressed in their Sunday best. The festivities end on the 15th day of the Lunar New Year.

Good Friday – Friday before Easter Sunday; usually in April
More than 10% of Singapore's population are Christians. The Christians observe Good Friday along with Christians around the world by attending church services and mass on this public holiday.

Labour Day – 1 May
Singaporeans celebrate the achievements of workers and why not? Labour Day is a day of rest for Singapore's fast-moving working population.

Vesak Day – 15th day of the 4th month of the Chinese calendar; usually in May
Budhhists commemorate Vesak Day, a holiday celebrated throughout Southeast Asia, which remembers the birth, enlightenment and passing of the Buddha. More than 40% of Singapore's population practice Buddhism; on this public holiday, devotees gather at temples bringing offerings, and parade the streets in a candle-lit processions.

National Day – 9 August
National Day marks Singapore's independence from Malaysia in 1965. The highlight of the day is the National Day Parade with a spectacular show of fireworks, choreographed dances, and a display of military prowess watched by all Singaporeans.

Hari Raya Puasa – Coincides with the end of Ramadan according to the Muslim Calendar
Singapore's Muslim population observe a month of fasting (*puasa*) during the month of Ramadan. In anticipation for Hari Raya Puasa which marks the end of the fasting month, Singapore's Geylang Serai area gets dressed up in festival lights and open-air markets. Muslims head here to pick up traditional costumes and snacks to welcome guests.

Deepavali – Usually between mid-October to mid-November according to the Hindu Calendar

Also called the Festival of Lights, Deepavali is one of Singapore's most colourful festivals. Head to Little India where the streets are bedecked with Deepavali decorations. The stalls sell flowers, garlands, snacks, and Indian outfits and jewellery, to celebrate the Indian New Year.

Hari Raya Haji – Around 70 days after the end of the month of Ramandan

This holiday commemorates the end of the Hajj pilgrimage. Muslims in Singapore observe the holiday by sacrificing sheep, goats and cows. In accordance with Muslim teachings, those with financial means should help the less fortunate; the meat sacrifices are thus distributed to lower-income families.

Christmas Day – 25 December

No white Christmases here in Singapore, but the island celebrates Christmas in a big way. Orchard Road is decked out in Christmas lights and magnificent Christmas trees while the stores offer big discounts. Celebrated by Christians to remember the birth of Jesus Christ, even non-Christians bask in the festive atmosphere, often holding Christmas parties with turkey, a sumptuous spread of food and good company.

GLOSSARY

Ayam lemak chilli padi	A fragrant dish of chicken served in coconut-based gravy spiced with bird's eye chilli.
Ayam bakar	Grilled chicken.
Baba	Reference to a male Peranakan.
Baju kurung	A Malay traditional costume usually for women, with a long-sleeved blouse and skirt.
Baju melayu	A Malay traditional costume for men usually worn to the mosque or during Hari Raya festivities.
Bak kut teh	Literally translated as meat bone tea; a spicy, fragrant soup dish brewed with cinnamon, cloves and star anise, combined with soft pork ribs.
Bao	Steamed soft buns, usually filled with barbequed pork and bean paste.
Batik	Clothes printed with motifs using a wax-resist dyeing technique; widely found in Indonesia.
Bibik	A senior female Peranakan.
Bagedil	A soft potato patty popularly sold as a side-dish at Malay food stores.
Briyani	Typically consists of basmati rice suffused with cumin, cloves, cardammon

	and saffron, infusing the dish with a rich yellow colour; usually served with meat and especially popular with Singapore's Malay and Indian community.
Cantonese	Associated with Chinese people who originally hail from Guangzhou in south China.
Char kuay teow	A dish of flat noodles fried with soya sauce, cockles and fish cake.
Char siew sao	Barbecued pork stuffed in a flaky pastry.
Cheong fun	Rice noodle rolls; popular versions are stuffed with shrimp and barbecued pork.
Daun teh	Malay for tea leaves.
Daun belinjau	Leaf from the Berlinjau tree.
Dahl	A thick Indian stew made from lentils, peas or beans.
Dim sum	A Cantonese term for light snack or refreshment; a popular Chinese eating option, *dim sum* restaurants serve dishes steamed in baskets, served in small portions and with spots of Chinese tea to aid digestion.
Feng shui	An ancient Chinese system of divination popularly practiced today to bring "good luck".

Five foot ways	Corridors or walkways on the ground level of a typical Singaporean shop house which were traditionally five-feet across; upper levels offer shelter and shade.
Gopuram	A grand tower often at the entrance of a South-Indian temple.
Har gau	A dim sum staple; a shrimp dumpling with a slightly translucent 'skin' made from wheat starch.
Hakka	Associated with Chinese people who speak the Hakka language; today, the Hakka people can be predominantly found in Guangdong, Fujian, and Jiangxi in China.
Hainanese	Associated with Chinese Associated with Chinese people who originally hail from Hainan island in south China.
Ikan bakar	Grilled fish.
Kampung/ Kampong	A Malay village or settlement in Southeast Asia, where residents live in simple wooden houses with thatched roofs.
Kaya	A green and sweet jam made from coconut, pandan leaves and sugar; usually served with toast.
Klang	Capital of Selangor, Malaysia.

Kopi tiam	Local term for coffee shop.
Kueh pie tee	A classic Peranakan snack; a filling of turnips, shrimps and carrots delicately placed in a golden and crispy flour cup.
Laksa	A Peranakan dish served with rice vermicelli, soaked in a fragrant coconut curry-based soup with slices of fish cake, cockles and prawns.
Lao puo bing	A traditional Chinese pastry also known as Wife's Biscuit or Sweetheart Cake; made with almond paste, winter melon and sesame, and flavoured with five spice powder.
Lontong	A compressed rice cake, usually eaten in bite-sized cubes.
Makcik	Respectful term used to refer to an elderly Malay woman.
Murtabak	A flaky pastry dish filled with mutton, chopped onions and eggs.
Muruku	A southern Indian snack made with rice flour and urad, a south Asian bean.
Nasi kerabu	Herbal rice hailing from Kelantan, Malaysia.
Nasi lemak	Steamed coconut rice typically served with dried anchovies, fried fish, cucumber slices, and chilli.

Nasi padang	Originating from Padang, Indonesia; steamed rice served with a wide range of meat and vegetable dishes.
Niu che shui	Literally translated as "Bullock Cart Water". Old nickname for Chinatown referring to a time when bullocks ferried water to Chinatown's residents.
Nonya chang	A pyramid-shaped glutinous rice dumpling wrapped in pandan leaves; popularly filled with pork, mushrooms and salted egg yolks.
Orang laut	Literally translated as sea people; a reference to the indigenous Malay inhabitants of Singapore.
Or luak	A Singaporean omelette dish of pan-fried oysters, flour and egg.
Otah	Mackeral fish paste wrapped in banana leaves and grilled over charcoal.
Papadam	A crispy cracker to be eaten alone or with Indian dips and toppings.
Pasar malam	Malay for night market; rambunctious markets found in Singapore's residential neighbourhoods selling cheap goods and snacks.
Roti prata	An Indian flour-based pancake eaten with curry; additional ingredients include egg, onions, or cheese.

Sambal	An extra-spicy chilli-based sauce commonly used in seafood dishes.
Sarong kebaya	A traditional blouse-dress made from sheer fabrics, silk, lace or brocade and the uniform of Singapore Airlines' stewardesses; *nyonya kebayas* are a variation of the kebaya design worn by the Peranakans.
Satay	Charcoal-grilled meats served on a stick. Widely available in chicken, beef and mutton and served with peanut sauce.
Sedap	Malay for delicious or yummy; give positive feedback to your friendly Malay hawker by saying the dishes were "sedap".
Syonan-to	Singapore's name under the Japanese Occupation during World War II or "Island of the Light of the South".
Teh tarik	An extra frothy mix of black tea and condensed milk made by "pulling" the tea between two drinking vessels.
Thosai	A crepe-like Indian pancake eaten with dips, curries and vegetables.
Wayang	Meaning theatre in Indonesian; in the local context, it refers to Chinese street opera.

ORO *editions*
Publishers of Architecture, Art, and Design
Gordon Goff – Publisher
USA, ASIA, EUROPE, MIDDLE EAST
www.oroeditions.com
info@oroeditions.com

Copyright © 2011 by ORO *editions*

SURPRISING SINGAPORE: 101 THINGS TO DO

ISBN: 978-0-9819857-0-1

Designed and Produced by ORO *editions* Pte Ltd, Singapore
Graphic Design: Davina Tjandra
Writers: Adeline Loh and Edwin Tam
Photographers: See Chee Keong, except page 208 by Tim Nolan
Editor and Project Manager: Joanne Tan
Production Manager: Usana Shadday
Production Assistance: Gabriel Ely
Project Coordinator: Christy LaFaver
Color Separation and Printing: ORO *group* Ltd
Text printed using offset sheetfed printing process in 4 color
on 128gsm premium matt art paper.
Printed in China.

All rights reserved. No part of this book may be reproduced, stored in a retrieval system, or transmitted in any form or by any means, including electronic, mechanical, photocopying of microfilming, recording, or otherwise (except that copying permitted by Sections 107 and 108 of the U.S. Copyright Law and except by reviewers for the public press) without written permission from the publisher.

Library of Congress Cataloging-in-Publication Data Available.

ORO *editions* has made every effort to minimize the overall carbon footprint of this project. As part of this goal, ORO *editions*, in association with Global ReLeaf, have arranged to plant two trees for each and every tree used in the manufacturing of the paper produced for this book. Global ReLeaf is an international campaign run by American Forests, the nation's oldest nonprofit conservation organization. Global ReLeaf is American Forests' education and action program that helps individuals, organizations, agencies, and corporations improve the local and global environment by planting and caring for trees.

This publication is supported under the National Heritage Board's Heritage Industry Incentive programme Hi2P.

25% OFF

Present this coupon to enjoy a 25% discount on admission to the Mint Museum of Toys!*

mint museum of toys

1 FOR 1

Present this coupon to enjoy 1-for-1 entry to all NHB Museums!*

National Heritage Board

I ♥ MUSEUMS

25% OFF

Present this coupon to enjoy a 25% discount on admission to the Red Dot Museum!*

red dot design museum
Singapore

20% OFF

Present this coupon to enjoy a 20% discount on admission to The Battle Box!*

THE BATTLE BOX

Terms and Conditions.

- NHB Museums include:
  Asian Civilisations Museum
  Memories at Old Ford Factory
  National Museum of Singapore
  Peranakan Museum
  Reflections at Bukit Chandu
  Singapore Art Museum
  Singapore Philatelic Museum
- Valid till 31 December 2011.
- Not valid for temporary exhibitions and other promotions.
- Non-transferable.
- Free entry for students, NSFs and seniors above 60 years old.
- Visit www.nhb.gov.sg for details.

Terms and Conditions:

- Valid till 31 December 2011.
- Non-transferable.
- Discount is applicable only for full-price adult, children and senior citizen tickets upon presentation of coupon.
- Visit www.emint.com for details.

Terms and Conditions:

- Valid till 31 December 2011.
- Non-transferable.
- Discount is applicable only for full-price adult tickets upon presentation of coupon.
- Visit www.legendsfortcanning.com/fortcanning/battlebox.htm for details.

Terms and Conditions:

- Valid till 31 December 2011.
- Non-transferable.
- Discount is applicable for adults, students, senior citizens and children tickets.
- Visit www.reddottraffic.com for details.

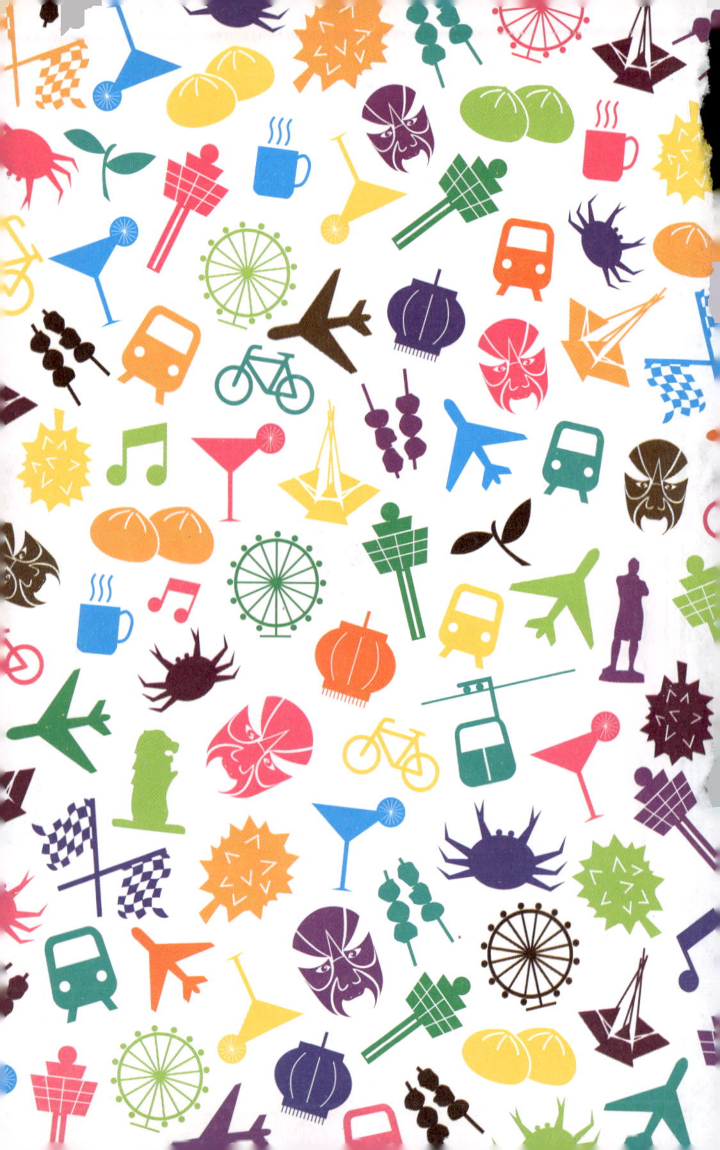